The HEART RATE MONITOR WORKBOOK

A Heart Zone™ Training Program

for Indoor Cyclists

Sally Edwards & Sally Reed

VELO *press®*

BOULDER, COLORADO USA

The Heart Rate Monitor Workbook for Indoor Cyclists
A Heart Zone Training Program
© 2001 Sally Edwards and Sally Reed

Printed in the United States of America

Distributed in the United States and Canada by Publishers Group West

International Standard Book Number: 1-884737-93-5

Library of Congress Cataloging-in-Publication Data
Edwards, Sally, 1947-
    The heart rate monitor workbook for indoor cyclists / Sally Edwards and
Sally Reed.
        p. cm.
    Includes bibliographical references.
    ISBN 1-884737-93-5
    1. Cycling—Health aspects—Handbooks, manuals, etc. 2.
Cycling—Training—Handbooks, manuals, etc. 3. Heart rate monitoring—Handbooks,
manuals, etc. I. Reed, Sally, 1948- II. Title.

RC1220.C8 E35 2001
613.7'11'0247966—dc21   00-054544

VELO
press®

1830 North 55th Street
Boulder, Colorado 80301-2700 USA
303/440-0601; fax 303/444-6788; e-mail velopress@7dogs.com

To purchase additional copies of this book or other VeloPress books,
call 800/234-8356 or visit us on the Web at VELOPRESS.COM.

Cover design by Paulette Livers-Lambert
Interior layout and production by Paula Megenhardt

Contents

Acknowledgments

This workbook would not have been possible without the encouragement and support of the following people:

The Bellevue Club Heart Zones Cycling class members, who faithfully came each week to test and develop each and every one of these workouts.

Sue Dills, who continues to inspire and encourage us with her vitality and competitive spirit.

Sue Matyas, for helping us see the bigger picture.

Joan Ritter, who helped take an idea and turn it into reality.

Betsy Herring, Abbie Morris, Carolyn Behse, Suzanne Strom Reed, Duane Reed, Dean Behse, and Scott Morris, who rode countless hours and miles listening to overzealous commentary on the benefits of heart rate monitors and heart zone training.

Dr. Stan Herring, for helping keep us in the saddle, training, racing, and living life to the fullest.

Scott Reed, for sharing his life with me (Sally Reed) and supporting the development of a dream.

Shawn Boom, for taking the Heart Rate Monitor for Outdoor and Indoor Cyclists and applying it to prove how effective it really is.

Kathy Kent and Jessica Menendez, for rounding up the support team and building the Heart Zones Cycling Training Company with us.

Deve Swaim, Chris Wentworth, Pietro Michelucci, Diane Lydon, and Dan Rudd, the partners and associates of the Heart Zones Company, for contributing to the application of the Heart Zone Training system.

Estelle Gray and her company, R and E Cycles of Seattle, Washington, for their support and sponsorships.

Caroline Dunn, for proofing the manuscript.

And, finally, Theresa van Zante, Amy Sorrells, and Mary Eberle, for riding on the VeloPress project team that put this workout book into your hands.

Training on your bike can best be accomplished by living a lifestyle of fitness and health. Jessica Menendez, Heart Zones Red Jersey Trainer, shows that heart with radiance.

Chapter 1
Why Cycle with Your Heart

Imagine being fit, strong, and in great cycling shape. Whether you are a beginner or an experienced rider, you know it's time to get on your bike and use it to reach your goals of losing weight, reducing stress, and developing competitive muscles. Success is addictive, and with Heart Zones Cycling you can ride across the finish lines of your training program in style.

We believe there are four parts to training successfully: (1) an effective *training plan* or program; (2) the *inspiration* and motivation to train, whether from well-defined personal goals or the sheer pleasure of training; (3) *support* for learning about training; and (4) feedback on your *results* throughout the training process. With a training plan, inspiration, and support, you will be able to see and enjoy the results of your efforts.

This book helps you develop a training plan and offers support for learning about training. While we provide some inspiring examples of cyclists who have set and achieved their goals, establishing your goals is up to you. As for the feedback on your results, that's where your new coach, the heart rate monitor, really shines.

In heart-based cycling or *Heart Zones Cycling*, heart rate or exercise intensity is measured by using a heart rate monitor. A heart rate monitor takes the guesswork out of determining your training intensity and provides valuable feedback in terms of recovery, overtraining, racing strategies, and overall health. In its purest form, a heart rate monitor is a biofeedback tool. Our goals are to help you use this tool correctly, to individualize your training to fit your goals, and to show how you can reap the benefits of smart indoor training.

Each of the workouts in this book is based on your maximum heart rate, and we show you how to determine that important number. Your heart sets the tempo and the pace during each workout, and your heart reaps the benefits.

The benefits of training together indoors on a bike lead to improved health and fitness.

Courtesy of Star Trac

What's the best way to practice Heart Zones Cycling? We think it's indoor cycling, because we have found that it:

- improves your "on road" training
- maximizes training time, making it as efficient, effective, and beneficial as possible
- allows control of the environment and protects the rider from extreme temperatures, wind, sun exposure, etc.
- eliminates hassles and dangers caused by inclement weather and poor visibility
- permits total concentration on technique
- lets the rider control exercise intensity to enhance fitness, prepare for rides through difficult terrain, or recover from high-intensity exercise
- offers the benefits of training with a group without the potential of being "dropped" or left behind
- provides the opportunity to listen to music, television, books on tape, etc.
- affords safety through avoidance of traffic, road hazards such as potholes and flat tires, and perhaps best of all, for those of us in frosty climates,
- gives a jump-start on the outdoor cycling season!

Chapter 2
Cycling in Your Heart Zones

Ready? This is in some ways the most important chapter of this book. So you have to promise to read it at least once, if only to ensure you have the basic information you need in order to start Heart Zones Cycling.

Here's the first important point to remember (middle-aged guys and gals, this means you especially!): Prior to starting any exercise program, it's important to have a physical examination. Men over forty and women over fifty should have a medical examination and diagnostic exercise test before starting a vigorous exercise program, as should symptomatic men and women of any age. If in doubt, consult your physician for clearance.

Please note that we are only presenting some of the most basic points on Heart Zones Cycling. For more details, see our book *The Heart Rate Monitor Book for Outdoor and Indoor Cyclists* (VeloPress, 2000).

Heart Basics

The first step to creating a more powerful training program is to get to know a little more about your own heart. This is heart-based training, after all, and you are a heart-based being, true? So getting to better know your heart—not someone else's!—in order to better work with it is key.

There are four heart basics that apply to everyone. The first heart basic is that as you put forth varying degrees of effort, your heart responds by varying its heart rate, which means that your heart rate directly corresponds to your level of exertion or effort. This effort is usually physical, but it can also be mental or emotional.

Second, when training, ideally, you should efficiently and methodically challenge your body. However, guessing your body's efforts on the basis of your perceived exertion alone can be challenging. "Well, I think I was breathing this hard when I was riding yesterday" just doesn't tend to cut it. Regulating your workouts via your heart rate, which directly corresponds to your effort and which you can measure absolutely, is much more of a "sure thing" for efficient training.

Third, hearts have a maximum number of times per minute that they can beat, called the *maximum heart rate*. Maximum heart rate varies from person to person and also varies for a given individual over the course of his or her lifetime. Among the influences on an individual's maximum heart rate are gender, age, weight, heredity, and lifetime (loss of) fitness.

The fourth heart basic is that if you know your own personal maximum heart rate, you can figure out what heart rates to train at in order to get fit and perform more powerfully. Research has shown that at certain levels of effort, specific training benefits occur, and these levels of effort can be measured by heart rate, relative to the maximum heart rate.

Maximum Heart Rate

Determining your maximum heart rate is pretty simple. Sometimes, in fact, it is too simple, so a word of warning seems appropriate here. Many mathematical equations that people use to determine maximum heart rate are of the one-size-fits-all variety. Because your maximum heart rate is yours alone, we recommend against most of these purely mathematical formulas.

For example, the following table lists the ages and maximum heart rates for some members of the Dutch national cycling team. Even though these are all top-level Olympic-class athletes, you can see that there is a wide variation in maximum heart rate that does not directly relate to age.

MAXIMUM HEART RATES AND AGES FOR DUTCH NATIONAL CYCLING TEAM MEMBERS

Name	Age	Maximum Heart Rate
Marco Gielen	24	180
Luc Wratwaar	26	188
Rene Godlieb	27	196
Helle Vullings	27	197
Annie Kerkhof	41	178
Anton Root	44	182
Cor Messing	51	182

The one mathematical formula that we do recommend is our version of one developed by Dan Heil, Ph.D. However, even this formula is best used as an estimate in order to perform other, more precise tests. (Note that bpm means beats per minute.)

Maximum heart rate (in *bpm*) = 210 − (half your age in years) − (5% of your weight in pounds) + 4 (for men only; do not add anything for women)

So, for Sally Reed, who just turned 52 and weighs 120 pounds, the formula looks like this:

$$210 - (0.5 \times 52) - (0.05 \times 120) - 0 = 210 - (26) - (6) + 0 = 178 \text{ bpm}$$

This is remarkably close to Sally Reed's actual, tested maximum heart rate of 180 bpm.

To calculate 5% of your weight, you can multiply your weight by 0.05 or take 10% of your weight (in Sally Reed's case, 10% of 120 pounds is 12 pounds), then cut that number in half again (for Sally Reed, that gives 6 pounds). The math is a little like figuring out a tip at a restaurant, but not quite!

MAXIMUM HEART RATE TESTS

Based on your estimated maximum heart rate, you can now move on to actually performing some tests to pin the number down further.

Before we begin, a note of caution: *Do not take self-administered tests if you are over thirty-five years of age, have been sedentary, or for any reason are in poor physical condition and have not had a thorough physical exam (including an exercise stress test) and obtained a physician's release!*

The Two- to Four-Minute Test Subtracting warm-up and warm-down, this test only takes about 2 to 4 minutes to complete. The test is easiest to perform on an indoor bike, but any bike will do. If at all possible, you should perform the test with a riding partner. Your partner should cycle with you throughout the test, setting the pace and verbally motivating you.

To begin the test, start with an easy warm-up of at least 5 minutes. Your goal during the warm-up is to get your heart rate to an estimated 60% of your maximum heart rate (multiply your result from the formula above times 0.6 to get 60%).

Without stopping, begin the test by gradually increasing your speed so that your heart rate increases about 5 beats per minute (bpm) every 15 seconds. At each 15-second interval, your partner should tell you the exercise time—as well as offer some encouragement!—and shout your heart rate as you both gradually accelerate. Every 15 seconds, your job is to ride harder and faster, with the goal being to continue increasing your heart rate by 5 bpm over every 15-second period.

For example, if you complete your warm-up and start the test with a heart rate of 130 bpm, every 15 seconds you should be at 135, 140, 145, 150 bpm, and so forth, until, even if you go faster, your heart rate no longer increases. You will probably reach this point within a 2- to 4-minute period if your partner has helped you set the pace correctly.

When your heart rate ceases to climb—even with increased effort and pace—you've reached your maximum heart rate. You'll know when you are there because no matter how hard you try, you can't get a bigger number on your monitor. At this point, you've reached your maximum heart rate and can end the test. Now you have your anchor point to set your zones—your maximum heart rate. *(Please see page 6.)*

The Highest Number Test This test is pretty obvious. If you've got a heart rate monitor and have worn it for a while, especially during hard workouts, use the highest number you have ever seen on your monitor as your maximum heart rate. Make sure it's the biggest reasonable number and not, say, 300 bpm, since you don't want to use a number that's been influenced by interference from other heart rate monitors, which does happen! If two people are wearing transmitters within receiving distance of one another, the monitors may pick up both signals and add them together or simply increase your neighbor's signal instead of your own. In any case, don't worry. Just move away from your pal or move your receiver to your opposite wrist.

HEART CYCLING

TRAINING ZONE (% MAXIMUM HEART RATE)	FUEL BURNING														
Z5 Red Line 90%–100%	135 → 150	140 → 155	144 → 160	149 → 165	153 → 170	158 → 175	162 → 180	167 → 185	171 → 190	176 → 195	180 → 200	185 → 205	189 → 210	194 → 215	198 → 220
	Max HR	Max HR	Max HR	Max HR	Max HR	Max HR	Max HR	Max HR	Max HR	Max HR	Max HR	Max HR	Max HR	Max HR	Max HR
Z4 Threshold 80%–90%	120 → 135	124 → 140	128 → 144	132 → 149	136 → 153	140 → 158	144 → 162	148 → 167	152 → 171	156 → 176	160 → 180	164 → 185	168 → 189	172 → 194	176 → 198
Z3 Aerobic 70%–80%	105 → 120	109 → 124	112 → 128	116 → 132	119 → 136	123 → 140	126 → 144	130 → 148	133 → 152	137 → 156	140 → 160	144 → 164	147 → 168	151 → 172	154 → 176
Z2 Temperate 60%–70%	90 → 105	93 → 109	96 → 112	99 → 116	102 → 119	105 → 123	108 → 126	111 → 130	114 → 133	117 → 137	120 → 140	123 → 144	126 → 147	129 → 151	132 → 154
Z1 Healthy Heart 50%–60%	75 → 90	78 → 93	80 → 96	83 → 99	85 → 102	88 → 105	90 → 108	93 → 111	95 → 114	98 → 117	100 → 120	103 → 123	105 → 126	108 → 129	110 → 132

Fuel Burning: **GLYCOGEN BURNING** (upper zones) / **FAT BURNING** (lower zones)

Heart Zones

Remember when we mentioned particular levels of effort that were relative to the maximum heart rate, and how training at those levels of effort provides wonderfully focused training benefits? Well, those levels of effort are not just specific numbers (for example, if training at a heart rate of exactly 104 bpm were to provide fat-burning benefits, but training at 103 bpm or 105 bpm would not!). Instead, there are entire ranges or zones of effort in which you can achieve specific training benefits.

For each of these examples, we'll be using Sally Reed's actual maximum heart rate of 180 bpm to determine her heart rate range in each of the five zones of effort.

ZONE 1: HEALTHY HEART

Even though it's the "easiest" zone, it is probably one of the most important zones of all. The Healthy Heart Zone is the first level where your exercise efforts provide health benefits, including lowered blood pressure and cholesterol levels, a decrease of body fat, and an increase of muscle mass. If your interests are to improve your health, especially if you are just starting a fitness program, the Healthy Heart Zone is the place to be.

Zone	Zone Name	% of Max Heart Rate	Fuels Burned	Calories
Z1	Healthy Heart	50%–60%	10% carbohydrates; 85% fat; and 5% protein	±4 calories/min.

If Sally Reed were to calculate her Healthy Heart Zone—that is, 50% to 60% of her maximum heart rate of 180—her figures would look like this:

$$0.50 \times 180 = 90 \text{ bpm}$$
$$0.60 \times 180 = 108 \text{ bpm}$$

So, Sally's Healthy Heart Zone is 90–108 bpm.

ZONE 2: TEMPERATE ZONE

The Temperate Zone is moderate and comfortable, just not quite as comfortable as the Healthy Heart Zone. Like the Healthy Heart Zone, this is another wonderful zone for burning fat calories, as well as even more calories overall, but it may not be quite as accessible for beginners on a fitness program.

Zone	Zone Name	% of Max Heart Rate	Fuels Burned	Calories
Z2	Temperate	60%–70%	15% carbohydrates; 80% fat; and 5% protein	±7 calories/min.

If Sally Reed were to calculate her Temperate Zone, her figures would look like this:

$$0.60 \times 180 = 108 \text{ bpm}$$
$$0.70 \times 180 = 126 \text{ bpm}$$

Sally's Temperate Zone is 108–126 bpm.

ZONE 3: AEROBIC ZONE

The Aerobic Zone is where relatively fit folks can get the most "bang for their buck." If you want it all from exercise—fitness, slimming, and increased performance—this is the level of effort where you want to be. Note that the Aerobic Zone, especially its high end, will likely feel like hard work to folks who aren't yet comfortable with Healthy Heart and Temperate Zone training, so we don't generally recommend that you hop right into an Aerobic Zone training program without building some fitness base first.

Zone	Zone Name	% of Max Heart Rate	Fuels Burned	Calories
Z3	Aerobic	70%–80%	55% carbohydrates; 40% fat; and 5% protein	±10 calories/min.

Here is how Sally would calculate her Aerobic Zone:

$$0.70 \times 180 = 126 \text{ bpm}$$
$$0.80 \times 180 = 144 \text{ bpm}$$

Sally's Aerobic Zone is 126–144 bpm.

ZONE 4: THRESHOLD ZONE

The Threshold Zone is where performance enhancements really come into play. This is not a zone where most people will spend long, steady workouts, but it is a place to visit for increased power and speed when it really counts. Why does the Threshold Zone increase your performance? Because it's the zone where you focus on increasing your body's ability to work by pushing through your *anaerobic threshold*. The anaerobic threshold is the point where your body switches from aerobic metabolism (that is, with oxygen) to anaerobic metabolism (without oxygen). Above the anaerobic threshold, your body quickly goes into oxygen debt and starts accumulating lactic acid. By increasing your anaerobic threshold, you increase your ability to metabolize with oxygen under higher levels of effort, thus improving your performance.

If you're less fit, you may recognize this as the "shortness of breath" zone, the one you feel when you dash up a set of stairs and regret the last three years' worth of cheeseburgers and fries. This is no joke: if you are unfit, your anaerobic threshold may not be anywhere near 80–90% of your maximum heart rate. In fact, it may be as low as 60%. If this is the case, as it is for many unfit folks, you can't train in the 80–90% Threshold Zone and should instead stay within aerobic intensity levels for all your workouts. Eventually, though, you'll increase your aerobic fitness to the point where even the Threshold Zone is open to you.

Zone	Zone Name	% of Max Heart Rate	Fuels Burned	Calories
Z4	Threshold	80%–90%	70% carbohydrates; 25% fat; and 5% protein	±13 calories/min.

The calculation for Sally's Threshold Zone is:

$$0.80 \times 180 = 144 \text{ bpm}$$
$$0.90 \times 180 = 162 \text{ bpm}$$

This puts Sally's Threshold Zone at 144–162 bpm.

ZONE 5: RED LINE ZONE

The Red Line Zone is the ultimate for athletic performance. It doesn't have anything to do with everyday health and fitness, and it's frankly very uncomfortable to train in. However, if you're like us and really enjoy pushing yourself beyond your limits, you will enjoy the Red Line Zone.

It's very important to note that because the Red Line Zone is completely above your anaerobic threshold, it is not a level of intensity that even trained athletes can maintain for long, and it is certainly not a place that most people should intentionally visit. Of course, most of us have unintentionally visited the Red Line Zone at one time or another, whether racing "out of breath" (literally, "out of oxygen") for a departing flight or after an escaped pet. Sound familiar?

Zone	Zone Name	% of Max Heart Rate	Fuels Burned	Calories
Z5	Red Line	90%–100%	90% carbohydrates; 5% fat; and 5% protein	±17 calories/min.

Here are the calculations for Sally's Red Line Zone:

$$0.90 \times 180 = 162 \text{ bpm}$$
$$1.00 \times 180 = 180 \text{ bpm}$$

This gives Sally a Red Line Zone of 162–180 bpm.

Establishing Heart Zones

The final step you need to take in order to train with your heart is to determine your own five training zones. Remember your maximum heart rate? Here is where it really comes into play. As we did for Sally Reed in the heart zone calculations, to determine your heart rate ranges for a given zone, multiply the percent of maximum heart rate times your actual maximum heart rate.

Congratulations! You've now mastered the basics of heart knowledge.

Zone Number	Zone Name	% of Max Heart Rate	Your Heart Rate
Z1	Healthy Heart Zone	50%–60%	___ - ___ bpm
Z2	Temperate Zone	60%–70%	___ - ___ bpm
Z3	Aerobic Zone	70%–80%	___ - ___ bpm
Z4	Threshold Zone	80%–90%	___ - ___ bpm
Z5	Red Line Zone	90%–100%	___ - ___ bpm

Chapter 3
Using a Heart Rate Monitor

Heart rate monitors are the first biofeedback devices to be widely available (other than mood rings!). With a heart rate monitor, you can be your own best motivator, personal trainer, and exercise physiologist. People around the world are discovering that a heart rate monitor is the best workout partner they have ever had.

The incredible service that a heart rate monitor provides is to make a seamless link between your body and your mind. You can determine your heart rate—and therefore your training benefits—at any moment just by peeking at your wrist. Even better, once you set your training zone into your monitor, it notifies you when you fall out of your zone! No more guessing your effort level, no more stopping a workout just to take your (usually highly inaccurate) pulse. Professional athletes have had access to this information for years, and now this simple yet potent training tool is available to everyone.

Before we go any further, we would like to present ten tips for training with a heart rate monitor.

Ten Tips for Training with a Heart Rate Monitor

♥1 *Select your heart rate monitor carefully.* Although there are many different models and manufacturers of heart rate monitors, there are only four basic types: Continuous-read monitors, zone monitors, memory monitors, and downloadable monitors. When selecting a heart rate monitor, choose features that match your personal needs. Prices range from approximately $50 for a basic continuous-read monitor to $400 for a top-of-the-line downloadable model. Generally, the more you spend, the more features you receive.

♥2 *Read the manual.* Take the time to learn to use your monitor—it's well worth the effort! It takes about 2 hours of dedicated time with your monitor and manual to learn how to push all of

Types of Heart Rate Monitors

Monitor type	Features
Continuous-read	Very basic and easy to read and use, continuous-read monitors simply tell you your current heart rate. They have no buttons.
Zone	These monitors let you know what zone you're working in. You can program in one or more zones and the monitor will beep if you are above or below your selected heart rate range. For purposes of heart zone training, you should probably have a monitor that at least performs this function.
Memory	Sometimes referred to as "programmable monitors," memory monitors are more high-tech and can store information such as time in zone, allowing you to recall the data later. They do not interface with a computer, but you will at least have some saved information you can use later for your training log.
Downloadable	Without a doubt, you'll get the most from downloadable monitors. They store heart rate samples or data for later downloading or manual entry into a computer.

the buttons and get it set up correctly for your first ride. Memorizing the functions and buttons when you're off the bike and in front of the manual will make using the monitor a whole lot easier when you're actually riding.

♥ **3** *Follow the 40-hour rule.* If you are new to heart zone training, don't expect to grasp how to make your monitor work for you on the very first day. It takes time, so be patient with yourself. It takes about 40 hours of ride time to become comfortable with your heart rate monitor, and it can be a steep learning curve for those who haven't fully embraced technology. But if you just sit back and enjoy the ride, you'll gradually get the hang of it and will truly come to love the power of the information the monitor provides.

♥ **4** *Be sure your belt is tight enough.* Erratic numbers often occur if your chest strap is too loose. A good-fitting transmitter will be more comfortable to wear as well as more accurate. As a general rule of thumb, start by fitting the strap around your waist and allowing approximately 6 inches of separation between the two end pieces. You can then slide the transmitter up around your chest, and it should fit tightly. The elastic does wear out, and replacement straps are available.

♥ **5** *Monitor by the numbers.* Your monitor tells you how hard your heart is working, and it measures it in beats per minute. Higher heart rates require more blood to be pumped. It's important to note, however, that it's not just exercise that raises your heart rate. Other factors, such as temperature, altitude, dehydration, type of exercise, state of health, or psychological stress can affect your heart rate as well. Heart rate is relative, not absolute.

♥ **6** *Believe the monitor.* Many monitor users think their monitors are broken. Typically, women say that their monitor doesn't work because the number is too low. Likewise, men say that it's broken because the numbers are too high. The monitor's numbers are almost always accurate. The problem is more often the individual's perception of how hard they are training. Working with your monitor—and trusting it—allows you to gain the benefits it offers.

♥7 *Use your monitor as a management tool, not a speedometer.* Many people just use their monitor to tell them if they are at, above, or below a designated heart rate zone. However, you can get more benefits and train less if you use it systematically to train for a goal. Use the information from your monitor to manage your heart rate training program, to keep you motivated, and to help coach you during the ride.

♥8 *Don't press the buttons underwater.* Your monitor is pressure-sealed from the factory to resist water. If you push the buttons when the receiver is under water, water can seep inside and damage or destroy it. Be careful in heavy rain as well.

♥9 *Don't change the battery yourself.* Changing the battery is something you should have the manufacturer do, and your manual will tell you where to send it for the work. Again, the unit is sealed under pressure, and when you reassemble it yourself, you may not get the same quality of seal that manufacturers do when using special tools. (Some units do allow you to change the battery yourself, but they will clearly say so in the user manual.)

♥10 *Buy useful accessories.* There are a number of items you can use to enhance and enjoy your monitor to its max. Check them out!

Wearing a Heart Rate Monitor

Heart rate monitors have three basic parts: (1) a receiver with a digital display, generally worn on the wrist and looking quite a bit like a wristwatch, (2) a transmitter that uses electrodes to measure your heart rate, and (3) a belt to which the transmitter is attached and that keeps the transmitter in contact with your skin.

The first step is to put the heart rate monitor on. The simple act of wearing the belt and transmitter will cause the receiver to display your heart rate, and this in turn will allow you to learn about both the monitor and yourself! (See tip 4 for directions on how to correctly wear and adjust the transmitter belt.)

The next step is to keep the heart rate monitor on for a full 24 hours, if possible. This may seem odd, but it's really an incredible learning experience. Glancing at your monitor's display throughout the day shows you many interesting things about your heart rate:

- Your heart rate will most likely vary with your body position, changing when you sit, stand, or lie down.
- Your heart rate will of course vary depending upon your state of physical activity, but you may also find that it will vary with your changing emotional or mental states!

- Your heart rate will probably be lowest first thing in the morning when you wake up; this is called your *resting heart rate*. As you increase your fitness, your resting heart rate will likely decrease over time. How low your resting heart rate is depends on your individual heart rate patterns; however, it's common to see resting (this is before you get out of bed and go the bathroom) heart rates in the 50s to low 60s.

- Your heart rate during the middle of the day, when you are awake but relaxed and not particularly active, is known as your *ambient heart rate*. It's interesting to note how different sorts of physical, mental, or emotional activities alter your ambient heart rate. For ambient heart rates, the rule is the lower the better. It's quite common for fit cyclists to have ambient heart rates in the 60s and 70s. If your ambient heart rate exceeds 80 bpm then you should review your exercise routine and the level of stress in your life. Ambient heart rates over 90 bpm can be indicative of a highly stressful lifestyle or other imbalance.

Sometime during that first 24 hours of wearing your heart rate monitor, you will also want to read the monitor manual. Because every heart rate monitor is a little different, we can't provide sure-fire instructions for setting up your monitor.

At minimum, you should understand how to set the time features on your monitor, as well as how to input the upper and lower limits of a heart rate zone. These functions are vital to using the monitor successfully for your training.

Additionally, learn how to work the alarm on your monitor. One of the most valuable features of a heart rate monitor is that its alarm will go off if your heart rate goes outside your targeted zone. For example, if Sally Reed wants to do a workout in her Aerobic Zone, she'll input 126 for her lower heart rate limit and 144 for the higher limit, since her Aerobic Zone was calculated to be 126–144 bpm. If Sally gets distracted and slows down, her heart rate may fall as well. However, the instant her heart rate drops below 126 bpm, the lower limit of the zone she has set on her heart rate monitor, the monitor's alarm will sound. This incredibly useful feature ensures that even the most distracted person cannot possibly forget to exercise in the desired zone.

Currently most heart rate monitors have many more features than these, so again, we encourage you to read the manual and wear the monitor. After a month of wearing the heart rate monitor while you train, you will be very, very comfortable with the monitor and will probably have learned a lot about your own heart in the process!

Chapter 4
Understanding a Heart Zones Cycling Workout and Training in the Health Zones

We would like to begin this chapter by introducing a few more basics: the basic rules of heart zone training the basic knowledge needed to understand heart cycling workouts and the basic benefits of training in the first two heart zones—the health zones.

Everyone should read the heart zone training rules and the workout discussion, but who should read about training in the health zones? Well, if your goals are related to beginning cycling, recovery (whether from an injury or from hard training), weight management, doing active rest workouts, or increasing the variety in your training, the health zones may be for you.

This is a good time to note that we assume you know what your goals are. Our years of experience have taught us that you will be more successful in getting where you're going if you have made a clear decision on where that is by establishing goals. Also, the more frequently you feel a sense of accomplishment or reach a milestone, the more motivated you become. So, set small, specific, reachable goals and try to make small, but frequent, fitness improvements. It works!

The Benefits of Low-Intensity Training

There are probably more reasons to train in Zones 1 and 2 (50–70% of your maximum heart rate, remember?) than for any of the other zones. That's because low-intensity exercise provides a wide variety of health benefits because it:

- Allows you to train longer, which means you can then receive more training benefits
- Makes up the recovery zones for those who train at higher intensities
- Improves blood chemistry, such as lowering triglyceride levels, improving blood glucose levels, and lowering cholesterol
- Raises self-esteem

- Can stabilize body weight
- Increases fat mobilization and use as a fuel source during exercise
- Decreases the risk of heart disease
- Builds muscle mass
- Lowers negative responses to emotional stress

For many people, the most desirable benefit of low-intensity training is fat loss or weight control. It's clear that losing body fat is not easy. There is no one method that works universally. Rather, for an individual who wants to shed body fat and gain muscle mass, a personalized fitness program is one of the most successful long-term methods. Cyclists using heart rate monitors have succeeded in losing weight because the information a monitor provides helps to reinforce that they are training within their personal "fat burning zones."

Knowledge of heart zones has shown us that a successful strategy for losing body fat and controlling weight is to follow the "longer and lower" way of exercise. Remember those heart zone tables in chapter 2? Each table showed the relationship between a zone and the fuels your body burns in that zone, as well as how much fuel (that is, how many calories) gets burned in the zone. The bottom line is that you may burn more calories in the higher zones, but as your body works harder, it stops burning fat and starts burning more protein and carbohydrates.

So, if you want to cycle to lose weight, start off by training in the lower heart zones and riding for longer periods of time at those lower intensities. This will allow your body to focus on burning fat as its source of fuel. With the combination of effort and time, most folks do succeed in changing their body composition by increasing their muscle mass and reducing their levels of body fat.

The First Fourteen of the Top Twenty Heart Zone Training Rules

What is *heart zone training*? It's what you're learning about and what you're going to do. It's the basis for Heart Zones Cycling, and it applies to any activity, whether it's cycling, swimming, tennis, yoga, love, work, or whatever. Heart zone training is the methodical use of your heart rate information—specifically, the heart zones and your maximum heart rate—to improve your life.

The following rules, like heart zone training as a whole, apply to any (and every!) activity. Here are the first fourteen of twenty rules for heart zone training (the remaining six rules are included in chapter 6):

1 *The First Rule:* You can best manage what you can measure and monitor. Let this be your mantra.

2 *The Individualized Training Rule:* You wear training shoes that are fitted to your feet, so your training program should be fitted to your heart!

3 *The Benefits Rule:* Training in multiple zones gives you multiple benefits.

♥4 *The "It's Broken" Rule:* Taking your heart rate by hand just doesn't work; it's broken, and the way to fix it is with a heart rate monitor.

♥5 *Performance Rule A:* A higher maximum heart rate does not make you a better athlete.

♥6 *Performance Rule B:* A lower maximum heart rate does not make you a worse athlete.

♥7 *The Fat-Burning Rule:* Oxygen must be present for significant amounts of fat to burn. To burn the most fat, you can use a heart rate monitor to ensure your heart rate never crosses over the anaerobic threshold.

♥8 *The Testing Rule:* You can use a heart rate monitor as the key testing equipment in your personal laboratory to learn as much as you can about how to perform your best.

♥9 *The Rate-Not-Pace Rule:* It's just as important to know your heart rate as it is your velocity or pace.

♥10 *The Precision Training Rule:* The narrower you can shrink your training zone, the more precise your training—and your training benefits—will be.

♥11 *The 5-Beat Rule:* If your morning resting heart rate is 5 beats above your average resting heart rate, drop your training for the day by at least one heart zone or take a full day of rest.

♥12 *The Inverse Relationship Rule:* As your training intensity increases, your training time needs to decrease.

♥13 *The Wellness Continuum Rule:* Training with your heart rate monitor is a continuum: from health through fitness to performance.

♥14 *The At-About-Around Rule:* Training near your anaerobic threshold heart rate helps to raise that number toward your maximum heart rate, and this effect increases your fitness.

How to Read a Heart Zones Cycling Workout

There are a few basic cycling terms you need to keep in mind for your workouts, as they are referred to throughout the 50 workouts included in this book. Some of these are also included in the table of Workout Abbreviations and Terms, which appears on the inside front cover of this book as well as in this chapter.

HEART ZONES CYCLING TERMS

Intervals Most of the workouts, especially those that reach into the higher heart rate zones, are based on interval training. During interval training, you alternate between short, high-intensity periods of effort and easier, low-intensity periods of rest or recovery. Intervals train your cardiovascular, muscular, and metabolic systems to be stronger and more efficient.

Resistance Workouts are driven by heart rate and individual training goals. For example, if your goal is to train for improved leg strength, you will use resistance (harder gearing) to reach your target heart rate numbers. If another cyclist's goal is to improve leg speed, pedal stroke, and efficiency, they will achieve their target heart rate numbers with *cadence*, that is, pedal revolutions per minute (rpm). A cyclist who has a heart rate of 150 bpm and who, with an all-out effort, is pedaling at a cadence of 60 rpm is probably using high resistance to train for strength. A cyclist with the same heart rate and who is pedaling at 125 rpm is probably training for improved leg speed and pedaling efficiency. Each rider has the same heart number, but different goals, different methods, and different physiological results.

Choice When the word *choice* is included in the workout, you must decide what to work on—strength, power, speed—as well as choose whether to cycle standing or seated. For building leg strength and practicing climbing out of the saddle (your bike seat), more resistance or harder gears are used at a specific heart rate. When focusing on spin or leg speed, less resistance or easier gears and a higher cadence are used. You may also choose to sprint to a certain heart rate within a given time to simulate a jump or fast start.

Cadence Cadence or pedal revolutions per minute (rpm) is key to cycling performance and body mechanics. In the workouts presented in this chapter and chapters 5 and 6, you will be asked to ride at various cadences. Calculate cadence by counting the down strokes of one leg for 6 seconds and adding a zero to get your rpm. Or an easier method may be to count cadence using the upstroke of one leg as it reaches the top of the pedal stroke. Some workout sequences include a 6-second number. High-speed cadence is good for recovery because it promotes circulation and refueling of the working muscle groups.

Form Your cycling form—your body position and pedaling smoothness—affects your training efficiency. It's best to minimize any extra movement, keeping your torso steady and letting your legs do the work. Your hips should not rock, bounce, or bob from side to side. Your shoulders should be square and your back elongated and flat. The abdominal muscles act as support while shoulder and neck muscles are relaxed. Hunched shoulders indicate that your shoulders are not relaxed.

Intensity Cyclists often mistakenly believe that more resistance (using harder gears) is the answer to getting fitter, faster, and stronger. Heavy resistance and big gears in the beginning lead to injuries down the road. Too much, too soon of any type of training can cause injury. Beginners need to honestly evaluate their fitness level and cycling skills and take it easy on the resistance or gearing. Remember that some injuries can keep you from training for a very, very long time.

Pedaling Pedaling with a smooth stroke in a circular motion while applying equal force through the legs to the pedals is the correct way to cycle. Sometimes it helps to imagine that there is a small pencil on the inside of each of your ankles and that your goal is to draw perfect circles with each revolution. The idea is to keep constant pedal pressure for the full revolution.

Music Music should be motivating and enjoyable. It is more important to choose music that sets a feeling or mood rather than to pick music just because it has a certain number of beats per minute. Special indoor cycling music that is choreographed to specific workouts is available.

Logging Keeping a training log can be motivating. It provides a way to permanently record vital information such as minutes trained in each heart zone, weight, resting heart rate, average heart rate, and more. Having a written record of your progress provides valuable insight into your training success. We have designed a companion book in which to log workouts called *The Heart Rate Monitor Log Book for Outdoor and Indoor Cyclists* (Velo Press, 2000). We have included a sample page from that book below.

SAMPLE LOG PAGES

DATE	SPORT ACTIVITY	DISTANCE	TIME	TIME IN ZONE				
				ZONE 1	ZONE 2	ZONE 3	ZONE 4	ZONE 5
3/15	Swim	100	30min	3min	15min	12min	—	—
3/16	Run	8mi.	1:30	—	10min	60min	—	—
	Swim	100	30min	3min	15min	12min	—	—
3/17	Rest Day							
3/18	Bike	18mi	1:15	—	9min	41min	25min	6min
3/19	Run	5mi	45min	9min	12min	28min	—	—
3/20	Bike	20mi	1:15	—	15min	60min	—	—
3/21	Run	6mi	55min	—	15min	30min	10min	—
Weekly Summary	Swim	2500	1:30	9min	45min	42min	—	—
	Bike	38mi	2:30	—	24min	1:21	25min	6min
	Run	19mi	3:10	10min	37min	1:58	10min	—
Year-to-Date Summary	Swim	8500	12:30	42min	6:45	8:42	—	—
	Bike	380mi	20:30	—	8:45	14:00	8:00	6:00
	Run	190mi	30:10	4:30	6:45	10:58	10:30	—
Notes:	I am really enjoying this training period. The feeling of getting fitter is wonderful!							

Key Workout Type	Average Heart Rate	Rating A to F or 1 to 10	Strength training time	Stretching time	% Fat/ Body Weight	A.M. heart rate	Altitude changes	Total HZT points
Interval	157	B	15min	20min	27%	63	1000'	125
					154 lb			
Interval	149	A	0	15min	27%	61	1500'	170
					155 lb			
Interval	149	A	0	15min	28%	62	0	75
Endurance	125				155 lb			115
SS		A-	15min	10min	28%	62	500'	230
Steady State	152				155 lb			
	165							
Speed	175	A	0	10min	27%	62	0	75
Endurance	125				154 lb			115
Hills	15bpm	A-	30min	70min	155 lb	62	3854'	970
		B						26,222
Notes:	Happy with consistency. Followed my training plan. Earned a B+, which keeps me motivated. Weight is steady.							

UNDERSTANDING A WORKOUT PROFILE

At the end of this chapter and in chapters 5 and 6, we present 50 Heart Zones Cycling workouts in a standard format. We describe each workout's goals and concepts, and then provide a chart that profiles the workout's pace and difficulty followed by a step-by-step workout sequence.

A workout profile illustrates the heart rate changes during a training ride. It is a workout-at-a-glance picture of the entire ride. If you were to train with a downloadable heart rate monitor and dump the resulting heart rate data into a software program, the profile of your heart rate numbers would resemble our workout profile.

There are different parts to a workout profile. In the sample that follows, named "Five by

Five," you can see that every 5 minutes, you change the intensity of the ride so that your heart rate changes by 5 beats per minute (bpm). The profile of this workout looks like a hill. The first half of the workout is like climbing the up part of the hill and the second half of the workout is like riding the down part. As the profile ascends, your heart rate increases. And, as it rises, you progressively ride in more difficult heart zones, from Zone 1 through and into Zone 4. Likewise, as you descend the hill, your heart rate slows and your intensity declines. On the down side of the hill, the workout is lighter and easier. Finally, you descend the hill all the way to the bottom in the cool down phase, during the last few elapsed minutes.

FIVE BY FIVE WORKOUT PROFILE

READING A WORKOUT SEQUENCE

A workout sequence describes how to do a given workout minute-by-minute, step-by-step. As the minutes elapse, you will be asked to make riding adjustments to either increase or decrease your heart rate. You will also be instructed to change body position on the bike. As you do this, you will ride through different heart zones. Take the time before you ride to complete the column labeled *Your Heart Rate* because these are the heart rate values that you will train at during the ride.

The *Riding Time* column represents the total amount of time that you sustain a given heart rate or stay in a certain range. In the Five by Five workout, you sustain each heart rate for 5 minutes and then change it up or down, according to the instructions.

How you make changes in your training intensity can be by your "choice," or we may suggest ways to change intensity that suit the goal of the particular workout. For example, if you are working on building leg strength, you will be directed to change your exercise intensity primarily by resistance and body position on the bike. By changing riding resistance these ways, you build muscle strength and ultimately riding power. The following workout outline has been completed to show you how to fill in your own form before you start to ride.

Sequence for Five by Five Workout for a Rider Whose Maximum Heart Rate Is 200 bpm

Elapsed Time (min.)	Workout Plan	Heart Zone	Your Heart Rate (bpm)	Riding Time (min.)
0-5	Warm up to bottom of Z2	2	120 bpm	5 Min.
5-10	Increase HR to maximum HR minus 50 bpm (bottom of mountain)	3	150 bpm	5 Min.
10-15	Increase HR 5 bpm, choice	3	155 bpm	5 Min.
15-20	Increase HR 5 bpm, choice	3	160 bpm	5 Min.
20-25	Increase HR 5 bpm, choice	4	165 bpm	5 Min.
25-30	Increase HR 5 bpm, choice	4	170 bpm	5 Min.
30-35	Increase HR 5 bpm, choice	4	175 bpm	5 Min.
35-40	Increase HR 5 bpm, choice (top of hill)	5	180 bpm	5 Min.
40-45	Decrease HR 5 bpm, choice (be careful to only drop 5 bpm in a controlled recovery)	4	175 bpm	5 Min.
45-50	Decrease HR 5 bpm, choice	4	170 bpm	5 Min.
50-53	Decrease HR 5 bpm, choice	4	165 bpm	3 Min.
53-55	Decrease HR 5 bpm, choice	3	160 bpm	2 Min.
55-57	Decrease HR 10 bpm, choice	3	150 bpm	2 Min.
57-59	Decrease to bottom of Z2	2	120 bpm	2 Min.
59-60	Warm down to bottom of Z1 (bottom of hill)	1	100 bpm	1 Min.

Heart Rate Ranges for a Rider Whose Maximum Heart Rate Is 200 bpm

Zone Number and Zone Name	% of Max Heart Rate
5. Red Line Zone	180 bpm—200 bpm
4. Threshold Zone	160 bpm—180 bpm
3. Aerobic Zone	140 bpm—160 bpm
2. Temperate Zone	120 bpm—140 bpm
1. Healthy Heart Zone	100 bpm—120 bpm

WORKOUT ABBREVIATIONS AND TERMS

The abbreviations used in the workouts are listed on page 22 as well as on the inside front cover of this book. Some of the terms included in this list have been described in greater detail at the beginning of this chapter. This table is a quick reference for you to use as you prepare for your workout.

UNDERSTANDING HEART ZONE TRAINING POINTS

You will notice that each workout contains a brief mention of the total heart zone training (HZT) points earned in the workout. Heart zone training points are an easy way to compare the difficulty of different workouts and, ultimately, to track your training and set training goals. (For more information on developing a HZT point–based training program, read *Heart Zone Training* by Sally Edwards [Heart Zones Publishing, 1996])

All you need to know here is how HZT points are calculated. It's pretty simple: You earn one point per minute of your workout, so first determine how many minutes or "points" you have, then multiply the number of points by the level of the zone you are training in. For example, on a 40-minute Zone 1 walk, you would earn 40 points (40 minutes x 1 = 40); for a 30-minute Zone 3 swim, you would earn 90 points (30 minutes x 3 = 90); and for a 25-minute Zone 2 ride, you would earn 50 points (25 minutes x 2 = 50).

Essentially, the more HZT points a workout provides, the more training you're getting. It's a revolutionary way of measuring total training effort, also known as "training load," and it's blissfully simple to use. Have fun with it!

Ready . . .

You are about to have some of the best rides of your life. Of the 50 different indoor cycling workouts, the first eight that you are about to experience take you in and out of Zone 1, the Healthy Heart Zone, and Zone 2, the Temperate Zone. These rides will help you become more accustomed both to your bike and to your new friend and coach, your heart rate monitor.

While these workouts may seem easy, you will probably want to try each workout on a different day. It might be hard at first to keep your numbers low and the workout easy, but please do follow your numbers. The reading on your monitor is accurate 99.9% of the time and tells you exactly what intensity of effort your heart is experiencing. So, if you think the rides are too easy and that you need to sweat and go hard, no matter how strong the urge, follow your heart, not your head.

Also, remember to stretch before and after you get on the bike to maintain and increase your flexibility. Warming up and cooling down are important elements of a workout, so don't sacrifice them, even if you have time constraints. Stretching, warming up, and cooling down are the parts of your workout that allow you to keep working out, year after year.

If you listen to the voice of your heart, you be able to hear it tell you more about who you are. When you listen to your inner heart speak, your outer world naturally and healthily changes.

WORKOUT ABBREVIATIONS AND TERMS

Abbreviation or Term	Definition
(%)	Percentage of maximum heart rate.
(a number)	For example, (8) means 80 rpm or a count of 8 revolutions in 6 seconds.
Active recovery	Easy, slow pedaling with little or no resistance (easy gearing).
AT	Anaerobic threshold. The heart rate number at which your body is producing more lactic acid than can be metabolized; also known as the lactate threshold or crossover point.
AT HR	Riding at, about, or around your estimated anaerobic threshold. Typically the highest heart rate number you can sustain for an extended period of time.
Bottom	The lowest heart rate number or percentage in each zone. Also known as the floor of the heart zone.
Choice	You decide "how" to change the intensity based upon your goals. You may choose resistance, gearing, cadence, a standing position, a seated position, or any combination.
Easy pedal	No resistance, easy gear, low rpm.
HR	Heart rate, usually expressed in bpm.
ILT	Isolated-leg training.
Interval	Alternating periods of higher intensity with periods of lower intensity or recovery time.
Max. HR	Maximum heart rate, usually expressed in beats per minute (bpm).
Midpoint	Halfway between the bottom and top of a heart zone. Usually expressed as a heart rate number or as a percentage.
Peak heart rate	The highest heart rate number during a workout period.
(R)	Resistance or gearing.
(Rec)	Recovery or decrease in intensity.
RHR	Recovery heart rate, usually expressed in bpm.
rpm	"Pedal" revolutions per minute. Also known as cadence. To determine rpm or cadence, count the number of pedal revolutions in 6 seconds.
Timed recovery	During recovery, count the number of heartbeats dropped in a period of time.
Top	The highest heart rate number or percentage in each zone. Also known as the ceiling of the heart zone.
TTHR	Talk-threshold heart rate. A narrow range of heartbeats in which you can still talk but you don't want to exert yourself any harder.
Work-recovery	Together, an interval consisting of an exercise bout or time period followed by a rest or recovery period.
Z1, Z2, etc.	Zone 1, Zone 2, etc.

Eight Great Workouts for Improving Your Health

WORKOUT 1. FIVE BY TWO

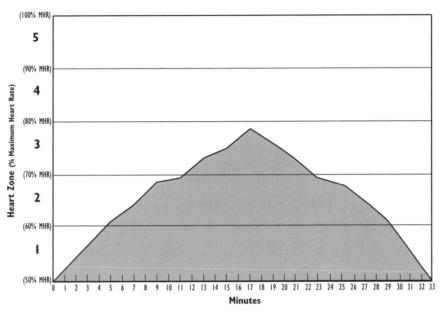

OVERVIEW

On many of the newer pieces of cardiovascular equipment such as treadmills, elliptical machines, and rowers, a workout profile chart like the one shown here appears on the console. Some pieces of equipment even give you the opportunity to select a setting whose workout profile resembles the workout that you want to experience. When you select a profile, the exercise machine is electronically programmed into a mode that varies the resistance in a way that changes your required effort to match the profile. The high-end machines have an additional feature called "heart rate control" that uses the data from your heart rate monitor to set the resistance. Most exercisers prefer these machines because they get an individualized workout programmed to match their heart rate response rather than a certain fixed amount of resistance.

Indoor studio or spin bikes have none of these features. Few have any electronics on them whatsoever. Rather, you must program the bike with your mind by making all of the adjustments to resistance, speed, and heart rate response. There is joy in simplicity like this. But, even more, there's the challenge of paying attention to the protocol to experience the workout. In this workout every 2 minutes you must be the programmer and increase your workload to increase intensity by 5 beats per minute (bpm).

DESCRIPTION

If you were to describe the workout profile of Five by Two, it is most accurately called a ladder. There is an uphill side to the ladder when your exercise intensity increases and a downhill side of the ladder when you decrease the resistance and your heart rate should drop to match it. Reaching the top of this workout ladder is only half the evenly balanced profile; coming down the ladder in a controlled manner for some may be harder until they gain more experience with their individual response to changes in intensity. With this protocol of changing intensity every 2 minutes, you can experience each of the levels on the ladder. Then, just as you achieve the desired heart rate, it is time to either boost or reduce your heart rate, depending on the direction of your travel and the elapsed time in the workout. Watch your monitor and focus on precision heart zone training.

STATS AND TIPS FOR WORKOUT 1: FIVE BY TWO

Zone Number and Name	Minutes in Zone	Heart Zone Training Points	Estimated Calories
5. Red Line			
4. Threshold			
3. Aerobic	10	30	90–110
2. Temperate	16	32	96–128
1. Healthy Heart	7	7	21–35
Totals	33	69	207–273

Tip 1: "By monitoring your heart rate, you can be sure you are safely and effectively exercising" (from Beth Kirkpatrick and Burton Birnbaum, *Lessons from the Heart* [Human Kinetics, 1997, page 49]).

Tip 2: Riding in the lower three heart zones results in improvement of health parameters, including lower blood pressure and improved blood chemistry such as amount and type of cholesterol.

SEQUENCE FOR WORKOUT 1: FIVE BY TWO

Elapsed Time (min.)	Workout Plan	Heart Zone	Your Heart Rate (bpm)	Riding Time (min.)
0–5	Warm up in Z1	1	_____	5
5–9	Increase intensity to max. HR minus 70 bpm	2	_____	4
9–11	Increase HR 5 bpm	2	_____	2
11–13	Increase HR 5 bpm	2	_____	2
13–15	Increase HR 5 bpm	2	_____	2
15–17	Increase HR 5 bpm	3	_____	2
17–19	Increase HR 5 bpm	3	_____	2
19–21	Increase HR 5 bpm	3	_____	2
21–23	Decrease HR 5 bpm	3	_____	2
23–25	Decrease HR 5 bpm	3	_____	2
25–27	Decrease HR 5 bpm	2	_____	2
27-29	Decrease HR 5 bpm	2	_____	2
29–31	Decrease HR 5 bpm	2	_____	2
31–33	Warm down to bottom of Z1	1	_____	2

WORKOUT 2. CHANGE OF HEART

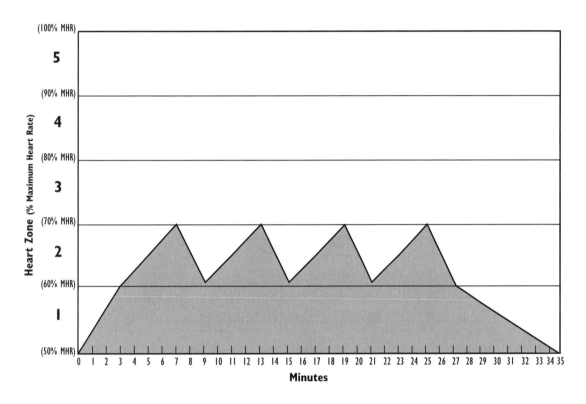

OVERVIEW

In March of the year 2000, those who traded in the equity stock market for Internet stocks took a change of heart. The high-flying balloon of Internet stock values deflated. This adjustment occurred in part because these companies' *burn rate*—or the amount and the utilization of their money sources for them to survive—was extremely high. They were simply metabolizing cash faster than what was reasonable. Stocks were considered overvalued and underperforming.

In contrast, a cyclist's *burn rate* on a bike has to do in large part with the amount and the utilization of oxygen and nutrients. To keep your burn rate efficient so you do not burst your energy bubble, training in the lower zones is ideal. Whenever exercising, the body burns a blend of the three fuels to create energy: protein, carbohydrates, and fats. Because Change of Heart takes place in the lower three heart zones, you burn a high rate of fat as the source of your energy. Remember, the higher the heart rate numbers, the higher the percentage of carbohydrates and the higher the amount of total calories burned, but the lower the percentage of fat burned.

DESCRIPTION

Riding a Change of Heart workout can be powerful because it is in the lower three heart zones. Most of the riding time is in Heart Zone 2, the Temperate Zone. It's named that because it is cool and comfortable, a zone you can ride in for long periods of time.

By riding in the lower three heart zones, you earn heart zone training points that lead to lower blood pressure, lower resting heart rate, lower percentage of body fat, stabilized body weight, and lower LDL cholesterol (the kind you do *not* want).

During the Change of Heart ride, by your choice of method you increase your riding intensity four times to the lower limit line of Zone 3, that is, its bottom. After kissing the Zone 3 entry heart rate, back off and ride gently. Change of Heart is a moderate-intensity ride that is ideal for performance riders as a recovery day and challenging for new riders to learn their heart rate response to different dosages of riding resistances.

STATS AND TIPS FOR WORKOUT 2: CHANGE OF HEART

Zone Number and Name	Minutes in Zone	Heart Zone Training Points	Estimated Calories
5. Red Line			
4. Threshold			
3. Aerobic	8	24	72–88
2. Temperate	19	38	114–125
1. Healthy Heart	8	8	24–40
Totals	35	70	210–253

Tip 1: To burn the highest number of total calories, train in the highest heart zones.

Tip 2: To burn the highest percentage of fat, train in the lowest heart zones.

SEQUENCE FOR WORKOUT 2: CHANGE OF HEART

Elapsed Time (min.)	Workout Plan	Heart Zone	Your Heart Rate (bpm)	Riding Time (min.)
0–3	Warm up in Z1	1	_____	3
3–5	Warm up to bottom of Z2	2	_____	2
5–29	[Increase HR 10 bpm and sustain for 2 min., then increase intensity (HR) to bottom of Z3 and sustain for 2 min., followed by an easy pedal (rec) to bottom of Z2 in 2 min.] Repeat a total of 4 times. Your choice of cadence or resistance (R), standing or seated	2 3 2	_____ _____ _____	24
29–32	Recover (rec) to bottom of Z2	2	_____	3
32–35	Warm down to Z1, easy pedal	1	_____	3

WORKOUT 3. CRISSCROSS ZONE 1 AND ZONE 2

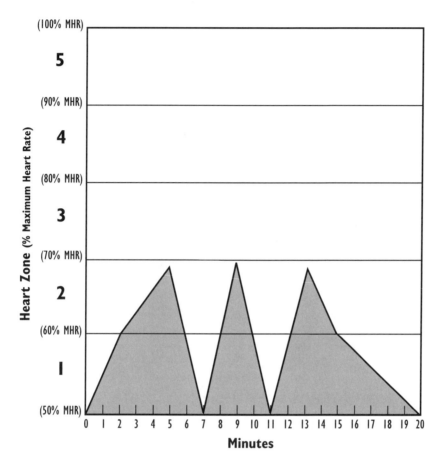

OVERVIEW

If you are just getting started on a fitness program, this 20-minute workout will help build an endurance and aerobic base. Zones 1 and 2 are the Healthy Heart Zones and lead to the development of a stronger heart muscle. In addition, by riding in low heart zones you are investing in such healthy changes as drops in blood pressure, lowering of serum cholesterol levels, stabilization of body weight changes, and improvement in your self-esteem.

The workout profiles are an easy way for a picture to serve for the words that they represent. Crisscrossing any one or two heart zones is a training ride of peaks, valleys, and rebounds. Each time you hit the heart rate number that corresponds with the top of the zone, decrease the intensity and allow your heart to recover until it reaches the bottom of the heart zone. When the bottom of the zone is reached, pick up the pace and increase intensity again, bouncing from the bottom to the top and then back to the bottom again.

DESCRIPTION

This workout will give you a feel for the two lowest-intensity zones, the Healthy Heart Zone (50–60% of your maximum heart rate) and the Temperate Zone (60–70% of your maximum heart rate). If this is your first time using a heart rate monitor or manually counting[1] your *pulse*, you may be surprised that when you ride these workouts, they feel different. The low heart zones are known as the *comfort zones* because they are friendly and pleasant. Additionally, low heart zone training offers a much-needed sanctuary of rest and recovery from higher-intensity training.

STATS AND TIPS FOR WORKOUT 3: CRISSCROSS ZONE 1 AND ZONE 2

Zone Number and Name	Minutes in Zone	Heart Zone Training Points	Estimated Calories
5. Red Line			
4. Threshold			
3. Aerobic			
2. Temperate	10	20	60–80
1. Healthy Heart	10	10	30–50
Totals	**20**	**30**	**90–130**

Tip 1: Use easy gearing or light resistance.

Tip 2: Focus on a round, smooth pedal stroke.

Tip 3: Study the five emotional heart zones. Learn more about them by logging onto the www.heartzones.com web site.

SEQUENCE FOR WORKOUT 3: CRISSCROSS ZONE 1 AND ZONE 2

Elapsed Time (min.)	Workout Plan	Heart Zone	Your Heart Rate (bpm)	Riding Time (min.)
0–2	Warm up to bottom of Z1, easy pedal	1	_____	2
2–5	Increase HR to bottom of Z2 (60% of max. HR) with (R) or cadence/rpm	2	_____	3
5–7	Increase HR to top of Z2 (70% of max. HR), choice	2	_____	2
7–9	(Rec) to bottom of Z1	1	_____	2
9–11	Increase HR to top of Z2 (70% of max. HR), choice	2	_____	2
11–13	(Rec) to bottom of Z1	1	_____	2
13–15	Crisscross[a] from bottom of Z1 to top of Z2, choice	2	_____	2
15–17	(Rec) to bottom of Z2	2	_____	2
17–20	Warm down to bottom of Z1	1	_____	3

[a] Crisscross: Increasing heart rate from the bottom of a zone to the top of a zone and back to the bottom.

---

1. Manually counting your pulse rate by applying pressure near an artery is known as *palpation*. This procedure is different from measuring the electrical signal of the heart as a heart rate monitor does. Rather, counting your pulse rate is a way of measuring the biomechanical heart signal.

WORKOUT 4. IRONSIDES

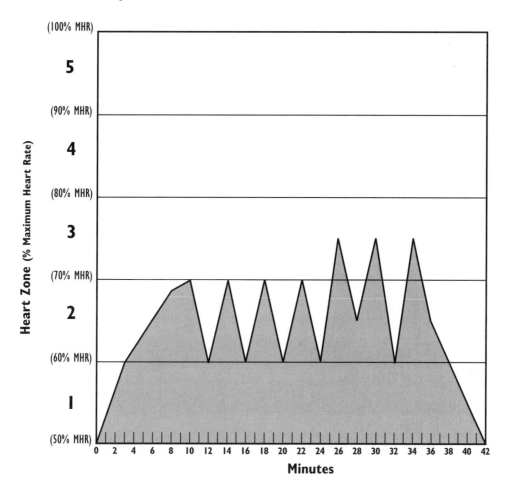

OVERVIEW

Like the warship that won every battle at sea, this ride will help you win as your heart muscle and your leg muscles learn to work together—to synchronize. When the two are working together, then both the iron of your quadriceps and the iron of your cardiac muscle are in unison. This condition of muscle synchronization is called *ironside training*. When you achieve this condition, you'll be able to recover quickly and enjoy training even more.

DESCRIPTION

This workout consists of seven easy intervals with the intensity ranging from 60% to 75% of maximum heart rate. The goal is to ride with relatively hard—like iron—resistance mostly in big gears for a 2-minute period. This builds strong muscles of iron. Next, recover to the bottom of Zone 2 (that is, to 60% of your maximum heart rate), which happens quickly when you are fit. As you get fitter, you may increase the work intervals by 1 minute, making the hard-riding period increase to 3 minutes, 4 minutes, or more but maintaining recovery time periods at 2 minutes.

STATS AND TIPS FOR WORKOUT 4: IRONSIDES

Zone Number and Name	Minutes in Zone	Heart Zone Training Points	Estimated Calories
5. Red Line			
4. Threshold			
3. Aerobic	14	42	126–154
2. Temperate	23	46	138–184
1. Healthy Heart	5	5	15–25
Totals	42	93	279–363

Tip: If your knees hurt, reduce resistance and increase cadence. Increasing both resistance and cadence develops power.

SEQUENCE FOR WORKOUT 4: IRONSIDES

Elapsed Time (min.)	Workout Plan	Heart Zone	Your Heart Rate (bpm)	Riding Time (min.)
0–3	Warm up, easy pedal	1	_____	3
3–6	Increase HR to bottom of Z2	2	_____	3
6–8	Increase HR to midpoint of Z2, (R)	2	_____	2
8–10	Increase HR 5 bpm, (R)	2	_____	2
10–12	Increase HR to bottom of Z3, (R)	3	_____	2
12–14	(Rec) to bottom of Z2	2	_____	2
14–16	Increase HR to bottom of Z3, (R)	3	_____	2
16–18	(Rec) to bottom of Z2	2	_____	2
18–20	Increase HR to bottom of Z3, (R)	3	_____	2
20–22	(Rec) to bottom of Z2	2	_____	2
22–24	Increase HR to bottom of Z3, (R)	3	_____	2
24–26	(Rec) to bottom of Z2	2	_____	2
26–28	Increase HR to midpoint of Z3 (R)	3	_____	2
28–30	(Rec) to midpoint of Z2	2	_____	2
30–32	Increase HR to midpoint of Z3 (R)	3	_____	2
32–34	(Rec) to bottom of Z2	2	_____	2
34–36	Increase HR to midpoint of Z3 (R)	3	_____	2
36–38	(Rec) to midpoint of Z2	2	_____	2
38–42	Warm down to bottom of Z2 then Z1	2 1	_____ _____	4

WORKOUT 5. RECOVERY INTERVALS

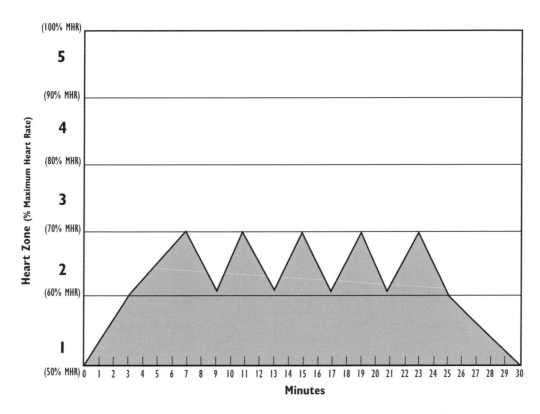

OVERVIEW

There are days when your legs need you to give them a break—a recovery day. Here's a way to use your recovery day as a way to maintain your fitness, burn a few extra calories, and just ride for joy without getting into the Threshold or Red Line Zones (Zones 4 and 5, respectively). This workout is also a great way to measure your "active" recovery (easy pedal) heart rate. This recovery interval is between 15–20 bpm, depending on your maximum heart rate numbers. This recovery interval is perfect for testing and to give yourself a break, as you will see. If you have more than 30 minutes to ride, then add several more intervals.

DESCRIPTION

A *main set* is that period of time in a workout when most of the training takes place. During the main set of this recovery workout, you will be riding in Heart Zone 2, between 60% and 70% of your maximum heart rate. Training in the low heart zones, Zones 1 and 2, help you develop a healthier heart. Keep the resistance low and "noodle" or "easy pedal" your way up and down each interval. Measure the elapsed time of each of your recoveries. Count how many seconds it takes for you to drop from the top of Zone 2 at 70% of your maximum heart rate to the bottom of Zone 2 at 60%. As you get fitter, it takes fewer seconds to recover because your heart is healthier. Retest your recovery time each month in a standardized way such as this one.

31

Another way you can do the recovery test is to measure how many heartbeats you drop in 2 minutes of easy pedaling (active recovery).

STATS AND TIPS FOR WORKOUT 5: RECOVERY INTERVALS

Zone Number and Name	Minutes in Zone	Heart Zone Training Points	Estimated Calories
5. Red Line			
4. Threshold			
3. Aerobic	10	30	90–110
2. Temperate	14	28	84–112
1. Healthy Heart	6	6	18–30
Totals	**30**	**64**	**192–252**

Tip: Make sure your recovery cadence is the same on each recovery and use easy gearing or very little resistance.

SEQUENCE FOR WORKOUT 5: RECOVERY INTERVALS

Elapsed Time (min.)	Workout Plan	Heart Zone	Your Heart Rate (bpm)	Riding Time (min.)
0–3	Warm up, easy pedal	1	_____	3
3–5	Warm up, easy pedal to bottom of Z2	2	_____	2
5–7	Increase HR to midpoint of Z2 (65%)	2	_____	2
7–27	[Increase HR steadily to bottom of Z3 (70%) for 2 min., then "active" recovery for 2 min. to the bottom of Z2 and sustain.[a]] Record the number of seconds to recover. Repeat a total of 5 times	3 / 2	_____ _____	20
27–30	Warm down to bottom of Z1	1	_____	3

[a] Recovery may be timed and a new interval started once the bottom of Z2 is reached. Count the number of completed work/recovery intervals in 20 min.

WORKOUT 6. ROCK BOTTOM

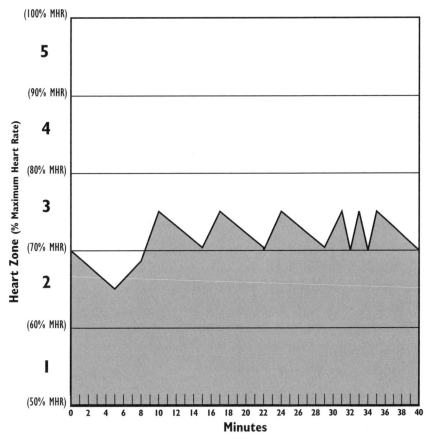

OVERVIEW

We have all had days where we've gone to the depths, hit our rock bottom. From down in those black pits, it can be a struggle that engages the heart to get out. One of the best ways out of rock bottom is to climb out step-by-step, pedal-stroke-by-pedal-stroke. Even Tigger in *Winnie the Pooh* couldn't bounce out of his rock bottom in one leap. When you crest the top and climb out of the hole, you can look back down and feel the accomplishment of being out. Next time, avoid riding the road that took you there.

One way to avoid rock bottom is to train with your heart. That's what this workout is about.

DESCRIPTION

This workout strengthens your cardiovascular system by pushing you to 75% of your maximum heart rate or the midpoint of your Aerobic Zone (Zone 3) with four challenging intervals. The first two intervals develop your sprint capability, and the last two intervals concentrate on leg strength and power. It might surprise you how fast 40 minutes goes by; because climbing out of rock bottom is a movement in the right direction, it is toward the positive. As the Japanese say in their expression *kaizen*, try to always take small pedal strokes toward improvement—constant, small improvement. *Kaizen* your ride by improving 1% a hundred times to equal a 100% improvement.

STATS AND TIPS FOR WORKOUT 6: ROCK BOTTOM

Zone Number and Name	Minutes in Zone	Heart Zone Training Points	Estimated Calories
5. Red Line			
4. Threshold			
3. Aerobic	18	54	162–198
2. Temperate	22	44	132–176
1. Healthy Heart			
Totals	**40**	**98**	**294–374**

Tip: Riding is a positive experience that can help you recover from personal challenges like those that negatively pull you toward rock bottom.

SEQUENCE FOR WORKOUT 6: ROCK BOTTOM

Elapsed Time (min.)	Workout Plan	Heart Zone	Your Heart Rate (bpm)	Riding Time (min.)
0–5	Warm up to bottom of Z2	2	_____	5
5–8	Increase HR to midpoint of Z2 (65%) with cadence/rpm	2	_____	3
8–10	Increase HR 5 bpm from midpoint of Z2, cadence/rpm	3	_____	2
10–24	Increase HR gradually to midpoint of Z3 (75%) by the following: [10 sec. sprint/50 sec. (rec) 15 sec. sprint/45 sec. (rec) 20 sec. sprint/40 sec. (rec) 25 sec. sprint/35 sec. (rec) 30 sec. sprint/30 sec. (rec) (Rec) to bottom of Z2, 2 min.] Repeat a total of 2 times	3 / 2	_____ / _____	14
24–29	[Increase HR to midpoint of Z3 (75%) by performing the following 1 min. interval: 45 sec. moderate (R) 15 sec. increase rpm] Repeat a total of 5 times	3	_____	5
29–31	(Rec) bottom of Z2	2	_____	2
31–36	Ups and Downs:[a] Increase HR from bottom of Z2 to midpoint of Z3, then (rec) to bottom of Z2 and begin interval again. (Count number of times up to midpoint of Z3 and down to bottom of Z2 in 5 min.)	3 / 2	_____ / _____	5
36–40	Warm down to bottom of Z2	2	_____	4

[a] Count the number of times you increase heart rate and recover in a set period of time.

WORKOUT 7. STEADY EDDY

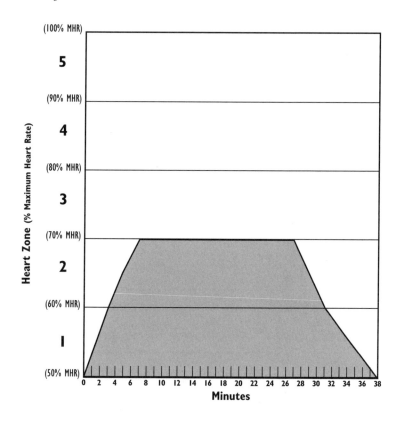

OVERVIEW

This one is easy and fun just like my training partner, Sally Edwards, the namesake of this workout. You simply ride according to how you "feel," holding a constant cadence and resistance in your *comfort zone*. Your comfort zone is a heart rate that you can sustain while still talking.

I (Sally Reed) know that Sally Edwards likes to cover her heart rate monitor when she reaches her comfort zone as she plays the game: "What is today's steady-state heart rate and today's comfort zone?" Try not to vary your cadence or intensity as you ride in your comfort zone for 25 minutes. Like Sally Edwards, learn to precisely know feeling and heart rate together by predicting a heart rate number and then peeking at the heart rate monitor every 5 minutes. Initially, you may be surprised at what your heart is really doing compared to what you "feel" it is doing, but with practice, you will be closer to the mark.

DESCRIPTION

Heart rate monitors are like the tachometers in cars. Tachometers give you quantifiable feedback on how hard your engine is working. Use your heart monitor as a tachometer to tell you what's happening during your ride. It can make a believer out of those who think that they know their heart rate without using a monitor. Perception of exercise intensity or perceived exertion is simply not accurate enough for training. For example, if you have a downloadable monitor or can borrow one, print out your heart rate during this steady-state workout to compare the plan and the actual profile. The two plots, if you are training on target, should match.

STATS AND TIPS FOR WORKOUT 7: STEADY EDDY

Zone Number and Name	Minutes in Zone	Heart Zone Training Points	Estimated Calories
5. Red Line			
4. Threshold			
3. Aerobic	24	72	216–264
2. Temperate	8	16	48–64
1. Healthy Heart	6	6	18–30
Totals	**38**	**94**	**282–358**

Tip: The workout profile is a graph that should match your riding heart rate numbers if you do the workout.

SEQUENCE FOR WORKOUT 7: STEADY EDDY

Elapsed Time (min.)	Workout Plan	Heart Zone	Your Heart Rate (bpm)	Riding Time (min.)
0–3	Warm up, easy pedal	1	_____	3
3–5	Increase HR to bottom of Z2 (60%)	2	_____	2
5–7	Increase HR to midpoint of Z2 (65%)	2	_____	2
7–32	Increase HR to bottom of Z3 (70%) or desired HR "comfort zone." Check HR every 5 min. and record	3	_____	25
32–35	(Rec) to bottom of Z2 (60%)	2	_____	3
35–38	Warm down to bottom of Z1 (50%)	1	_____	3

WORKOUT 8. FIVE BY FIVE

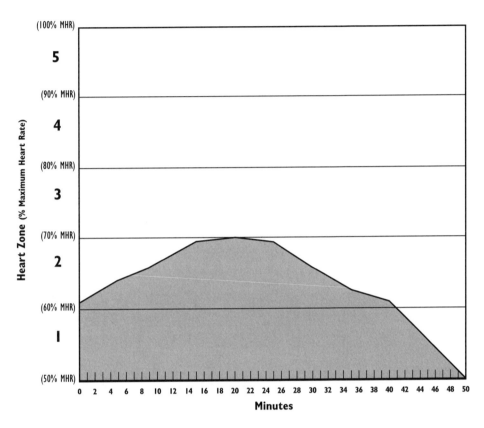

OVERVIEW

Equating profuse sweating with fitness improvement may at first seem to be intuitive to getting fit. It's not. Taking it easy is key to getting fitter. Often, an individual says to us, "I am training harder than ever before and getting slower." There are many reasons to attribute to that remark, and one of those is insufficient amount of recovery workouts. Five by Five is a low-intensity recuperative ride. Unfortunately, heart-healthy rides like Five by Five rarely get the attention they deserve because they do not fall into the paradigm of "no pain, no gain." It may only take the first injury or overtraining experience to understand and respect Five by Five. Ride it and watch yourself get fitter and healthier.

DESCRIPTION

This workout is a total of 50 minutes of riding time. It is ideal training for anyone who is just starting a cycle training program. It's also an ideal way to get a fair dosage of "R and R"—recovery and relaxation—while still earning heart zone training points. The workout plan is to ride up and down a 5-bpm ladder in comfort and with joy. During each 5-bpm increment you may select the mode of heart rate change. Change your heart rate with cadence, resistance, or body position such as alternating standing with seated positions on the bike. This is a training ride that does not beat you up, wipe you out, or negatively challenge your immunity system like the high, hot training rides in Zone 4 and Zone 5. Rather, this is a time to be social and get to know your fellow rider. For those of a more meditative disposition, it can also be a time to focus on a quiet mind, eliminating the constant chatter of monkey talk—Buddhists call one's inside talk "monkey mind." Whichever is your method, ride Five by Five with your emotional and physical heart. It has probably earned a day of it.

STATS AND TIPS FOR WORKOUT 8: FIVE BY FIVE

Zone Number and Name	Minutes in Zone	Heart Zone Training Points	Estimated Calories
5. Red Line			
4. Threshold			
3. Aerobic	5	15	45–55
2. Temperate	40	80	240–320
1. Healthy Heart	5	5	15–25
Totals	**50**	**100**	**300–400**

Tip 1: Change body positions often and try different interval techniques like isolated-leg training (a method of working just one leg at a time). During isolated-leg training, you pedal with one leg at a time, resting the other on a box or stool. You may also choose to keep both feet in the pedal cages or clipped onto the pedals and allow one leg to relax while the other leg does the work.

Tip 2: According to his holiness the Dalai Lama, the spiritual leader of Tibet, the first step to change is learning. Ride this workout as a way to learn more about your internal self. For more information, read the book the *Art of Happiness: A Handbook for Living* by the Dalai Lama and Howard C. Cutler, M.D. (Riverhead Books, 1998).

SEQUENCE FOR WORKOUT 8: FIVE BY FIVE

Elapsed Time (min.)	Workout Plan	Heart Zone	Your Heart Rate (bpm)	Riding Time (min.)
0–5	Warm up to bottom of Z2 (60%)	2	_____	5
5–10	Increase HR 5 bpm, (R) or increase cadence/rpm	2	_____	5
10–15	Increase HR 5 bpm, choice. Change hand positions	2	_____	5
15–20	Increase HR 5 bpm, (R), try standing and seated	2	_____	5
20–25	Increase HR 5 bpm, sprint with (R), then sustain (70%)	3	_____	5
25–30	Decrease HR 5 bpm, (R), isolated-leg training[a] (ILT), alternate legs	2	_____	5
30–35	Decrease HR 5 bpm, choice	2	_____	5
35–40	Decrease HR 5 bpm, choice	2	_____	5
40–45	Decrease HR 5 bpm, choice	2	_____	5
45–50	Decrease HR 5 bpm, warm down	1	_____	5

[a]Pedal with only one leg; rest the other on a box or stool. You may also rest it on the bike frame if you are riding a spin bike or simply keep your feet in the pedals and allow one leg to relax while the other does the work.

Chapter 5
Training in the Fitness Heart Zones

The middle three heart zones, Zones 2, 3, and 4, are frequently referred to as the "fitness zones" because by training within them you improve your measurable fitness level. Each heart zone provides a different set of fitness benefits, and you can maximize your workout benefits by riding in different heart zones, thus gaining the advantages of each zone.

The time you invest in the fitness zones will be richly rewarded. Because these are all zones where your body is able to use oxygen, the main benefit that you receive is an improvement in your aerobic capacity—the ability of your heart and lungs to absorb and use oxygen efficiently. The practical result is the ability to ride your bike farther, faster, and at lower heart rates for the same amount of elapsed time. Some of the other benefits of moderate intensity aerobic training include:

- Improvement in your ability to process oxygen
- Enhancement of your heart's ability to pump blood
- Increase in the number of mitochondria, the energy factories inside your muscles
- Increased efficiency in delivering oxygen and nutrients to your muscles
- Greater number and size of vessels that carry blood to your heart and other muscles
- Lower resting and ambient heart rates
- Protection from the degenerative process of heart disease

Fit and Firm for Life

Many folks would like to drop that last 5 or 10 pounds of body fat while simultaneously maintaining their muscle mass or even improving it. Those last few pounds are some of the most difficult because the body likes to remain at homeostasis—that is, it likes to stay at a set weight point.

One of the ways of getting lean is to burn more fat. To burn the highest possible amount of fat per minute of riding, you'll need to know your heart rate at the crossover point from aerobic to anaerobic metabolism (your anaerobic threshold heart rate). The closer you are to this heart rate, the higher the total amount of fat that you burn during your ride. Remember, if you pass your anaerobic threshold, you won't burn any additional fat as a source of energy. To determine your anaerobic threshold heart rate, use the Anaerobic Threshold Test described in Rule 15 in the section called The Rest of the Top 20 Heart Zone Training Rules in chapter 6.

Another way to get lean is to determine how many calories you typically burn when you ride. To make an estimate of the fuel that you use during a workout, simply multiply the number of calories burned per minute times the number of minutes you spend in each of the zones. The following table provides an example of a rider who trains a total of 180 minutes (3 hours) per week, spending different amounts of time in each of the different heart zones.

CALORIES BURNED FOR A RIDER
WHO TRAINS 180 MINUTES PER WEEK

Zone	Ride Time (min.)	Calories Burned per Minute	Total Calories Burned
5	10	17	170
4	25	13	325
3	100	10	1000
2	25	7	175
1	20	4	80
Total	180 minutes		1750 calories per week

If you are interested, you can also calculate the relative percentage of fuels that you typically burn when riding. To absolutely and precisely know the fuels your body uses requires some very sophisticated tests that simply aren't practical for most folks to have. You can, however, create an estimate of fuels that you use during a workout. In order to determine how many calories you burn are from fat and how many are from carbohydrates, for example, track the time spent in the various zones during your workout, and then using the percentages discussed in the heart zone descriptions in chapter 2, multiply the total calories burned by the percentages of calories burned in each zone.

The simplest way to shed those final few pounds is to channel your outgoing energy into activities like riding in the fitness zones and then use your incoming energy to manage your diet. With some effort and time, this energy shifting leads to a long-term reduction of fat weight and increase in muscle weight.

Heartfelt Changes in Heart Rate

To use a heart rate monitor effectively, you need to understand the various factors that can affect your heart rate. At any given time, one or more of these may lower or raise the results given by the heart rate monitor.

INTERNAL BODY CHANGES

Almost any substance taken into the body affects the normal balance of the body (its homeostasis). For example, beta-blockers, a common prescription drug for high blood pressure, can cause a drop in heart rate. This is also true of depressants like barbiturates, tranquilizers, and alcohol. Many pulmonary drugs, on the other hand, cause an increase in heart rate. And stimulants like caffeine, nicotine, methamphetamines, cocaine, and PCP also increase heart rate.

Lack of sleep, irritability, and rapid changes in blood chemistry (blood sugar levels, for example) can both raise and lower your heart rate. While emotions like anger, fear, and anxiety cause an increase in your heart rate, depression usually results in a lowering of heart rate.

ENVIRONMENTAL CONDITIONS

Heart rate is also affected by external stresses on the body, such as heat, humidity, cold, wind, altitude, and air quality. With each stress, different compensatory changes occur in the body. An adjustment in the beat of the heart is one of them.

Triathletes racing at the Hawaii Ironman face numerous harsh environmental conditions while racing in one of the most strenuous events in the world. As a result, top athletes use monitors to learn key information on how their bodies are responding to the conditions and the duration of this high-intensity event. At one time or another, you'll experience each of these same changes in your environment. It's going to affect you and your heart rate, so be prepared. The chart on page 43 describes some specific environmental stresses and how they can affect your heart rate.

NEURAL AND HORMONAL EFFECTS

Although the causes of neural and hormonal effects on your heart rate are complex to explain, you only really need to know that you have little control over your body's responses in these areas. A combination of neural and chemical components regulates heart rate and other heart functions, and the central nervous system plays the greatest role in control over heart rate during exercise. When you start to move, the system sends impulses through the cardiovascular center in the brain, causing a coordinated and quick response of the heart and the blood vessels.

GENETICS

The genes you inherited are responsible for much in your life, and they affect your heart rate, too. Based on our current knowledge, it appears your genetic makeup determines about 50% of the value of your maximum heart rate. So, if both of your parents have a low maximum heart rate, the odds are that you will.

LEVEL OF FITNESS

The fitter you are the less often your heart contracts, thus saving heartbeats. When well trained, your ambient and resting heart rates drop by as much as 30 bpm. When extended over a lifetime of fitness, you can save hundreds of thousands of heartbeats.

Interestingly, body composition or body type does not affect heart rate measurements. However, your body's state—whether your body is fatigued or rested—can affect heart rate measurements.

MODE OF EXERCISE

The type of exercise you do is one of the most significant factors affecting maximum and training heart rates. Maximum and training heart rates are both sport-specific. Generally, a higher training heart rate is attained when more muscle mass is used for the exercise. The higher heart rate numbers occur during sports that use both lower and upper muscle groups simultaneously, such as cross-country skiing. Heart rates are lowest when the body is in a horizontal position or in cool temperatures, as when swimming.

Heart rate and change in heart rate are affected by many factors. The heart takes into account all of these situations and conditions when it sets the frequency of the beat. You can't change all of the factors that affect heart rate, but your monitor will help you stay informed of your body's response—or lack thereof—so you can plan accordingly.

Set ...

By now you are familiar with your bike, your monitor, and training in two of the lower heart zones. Now it's time to pick up the pace and the rate. The next fifteen rides are more challenging, and you are guaranteed to break a sweat and ride to the point where talking is difficult.

Here are a few suggestions to make these workouts more meaningful:

1 Ride with lively music. The beat of the music and that of your heartbeat doesn't necessarily have to match. You will want to choose music that motivates you and sets a feeling or mood.

2 Breathe deeply and focus on the time you are breathing out, exhaling. Breathing is important in Zone 2 through Zone 4. Deep breathing is better on a bike than shallow, short, quick breaths.

3 Remember to take advantage of the three different ways to increase and decrease heart rate on your indoor bike: body position, cadence, and resistance. As you ride, play with these variables to change the beat of your heart.

One of the workout experiences the heart loves most is variability or frequent small changes. If you give your heart variety and fun, it will respond by pumping more blood, by strengthening itself, and by lowering your risk of most types of heart disease. You can build a stronger heart and healthier lungs by working out in the fitness zones.

Effects of Environmental Stress

Type of Stress	Specific Stress	Heart Rate Changes	Explanation
Thermal Stress	Heat gain (also applies to the heat gained from eating)	Elevated	Changes in heart rate are the result of changes in the core body temperature. Dressing appropriately is the most important consideration to maintain or reduce the body's core temperature. Dehydration causes heart rate to increase.
	Heat loss	Lowered	Thermoregulation adjustments result in improved exercise capacity to heat exposure but minimally to cold stress. This generally takes about 10 days. Shivering can increase the heart rate significantly and increase core temperature. Considerable water can be lost from the respiratory tract during cold exposure when exercising, which results in elevated heart rates.
Humidity	Dry air	Elevated	The water content in the ambient air affects the amount of water lost through sweating. In dry air, sweating can be profuse and result in a decrease in your blood volume leading to dehydration. Each 1 pound of body weight loss corresponds to about 15 ounces (450 milliliters) of dehydration. Still, hot dry climates are easier to tolerate than humid ones because evaporation of sweat, and thus cooling, can be achieved.
	Highly moist air	Elevated	Exercising in high humidity challenges the thermoregulatory system because the large sweat loss contributes little to evaporative cooling. Sweat does not cool the skin; evaporation of sweat cools the skin. Increased blood flow to the skin for sweating increases heart rate whether or not the sweating is effective at cooling.
Wind	Wind chill	Lowered and Elevated	Wind caused by physical movement or air movement magnifies heat loss as the warmer insulating air on the skin is continually replaced by cooler, ambient air. Wind causes heat to decrease and hence heart rate to stay lower. Wind chill factor is an index that shows the effect of wind velocities on bare skin for different temperatures.
Altitude	High	Lowered maximum and training heart rates	There is a progressive reduction in the amount of oxygen and its partial pressure as altitude increases. As a result, the heart beats faster to compensate for less oxygen per breath. Maximum heart rate drops with increases in altitude approximately one beat per 1,000 feet of altitude gain. The acclimatization process provides some relief from the effects of altitude, resulting in improved tolerance to altitude hypoxia.

Fifteen Great Workouts for Improving Your Fitness

WORKOUT 9. TALK IS CHEAP

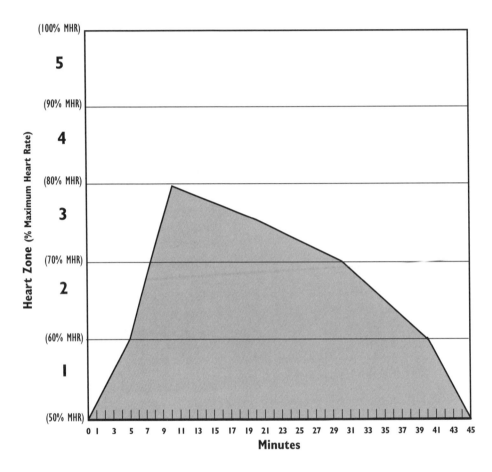

OVERVIEW

Some of us talk aloud, outside. Others have a running stream of conversation on the inside, in our minds. Some of us do both, simultaneously. Again we remind you that Buddhists call the inside talk "monkey mind." This workout is about letting your monkey mind out by training at your talk-threshold heart rate or what Heart Zones Cycling riders call the TTHR. Training at your TTHR is typically within the Aerobic Zone (Zone 3), so you not only have the reward of letting the internal stream of mental thought out, you also consume lots of oxygen and calories at the same time.

DESCRIPTION

Your talk-threshold heart rate or TTHR is a very narrow, skinny, thin range of heartbeats that perches on the threshold of heart rates just before talking concedes to the need for air for breathing. At this heart rate point, you feel that you can still talk, but you don't want to exert yourself any harder. Note the heart rate in beats per minutes (bpm) that closely resembles this point and write it down in your log. As you get fitter, your TTHR changes; the heart rate number goes up, and you are still able to maintain a conversation and hold a higher working heart rate. If you can let your monkey mind go at the same time, you will discover the bliss of riding.

STATS AND TIPS FOR WORKOUT 9: TALK IS CHEAP

Zone Number and Name	Minutes in Zone	Heart Zone Training Points	Estimated Calories
5. Red Line			
4. Threshold	10	40	120—140
3. Aerobic	20	60	180—220
2. Temperate	7	14	42—56
1. Healthy Heart	8	8	24—40
Totals	**45**	**122**	**366—456**

Tip: Every time you check your monitor, talk. If you can say a couple of sentences and still breathe, you are at the right TTHR.

SEQUENCE FOR WORKOUT 9: TALK IS CHEAP

Elapsed Time (min.)	Workout Plan	Heart Zone	Your Heart Rate (bpm)	Riding Time (min.)
0—5	Warm up, easy pedal, to bottom of Z1	1	_____	5
5—10	Increase HR with cadence/rpm to top of Z2	2	_____	5
10—20	Increase HR to 5 bpm above estimated TTHR and sustain, choice	3/4	_____	10
20—30	Decrease HR to TTHR and sustain, choice	3/4	_____	10
30—40	Decrease HR to 5 bpm below TTHR and sustain, choice	3	_____	10
40—42	Decrease HR to bottom of Z2, easy pedal	2	_____	2
42—45	Decrease HR to Z1, warm down, easy pedal	1	_____	3

WORKOUT 10. THE CHAIN GANG

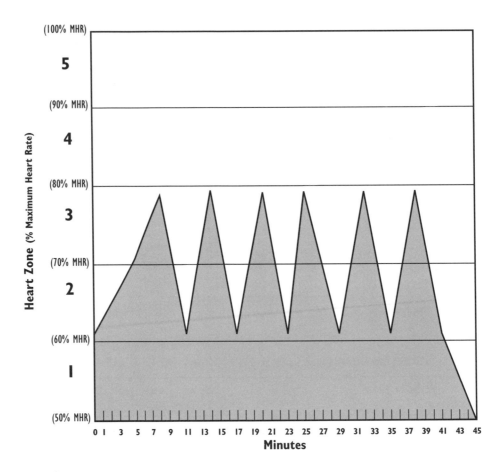

OVERVIEW

Ever feel the weight of that iron ball that's figuratively attached to your leg that keeps you from running away from your own incarceration? It's time to ride away from the chain and the gang of reasons that keeps you tied down. This ride breaks you free from the ball-and-chain lifestyle. This is a breakaway from the what's-holding-you-back prison. It is a freedom ride.

DESCRIPTION

This is one of our favorite 45-minute workouts because you cross two zones and experience the results of getting fitter, which is known as "the positive training effect." This workout is a grand tour of the two most scenic heart zones, Zone 2 and Zone 3. You will feel better about yourself after the ride than before the ride. It's a calorie consuming and oxygen-burning work-out. By training in these two fitness zones, you will get fitter and faster. The exercise high that often develops as you travel through Zone 3 results in mood improvement, reduction in anxiety, and improved appetite control. The physiological benefits leave a smile on your face that lasts for hours. Throw off your chain and join a new gang of fitness folks who love to train on their bikes with their hearts.

STATS AND TIPS FOR WORKOUT 10: THE CHAIN GANG

Zone Number and Name	Minutes in Zone	Heart Zone Training Points	Estimated Calories
5. Red Line			
4. Threshold			
3. Aerobic	23	69	207–253
2. Temperate	21	42	126–168
1. Healthy Heart	1	1	3–5
Totals	**45**	**112**	**336–426**

Tip: Try pedaling more horizontally through the bottom and top parts of the stroke. This approach smoothes out your stroke, recruits more muscle fibers, and provides you with enhanced power output.

SEQUENCE FOR WORKOUT 10: THE CHAIN GANG

Elapsed Time (min.)	Workout Plan	Heart Zone	Your Heart Rate (bpm)	Riding Time (min.)
0–5	Warm up to bottom of Z2	2	_____	5
5–8	Increase HR with resistance (R) or cadence/rpm to bottom of Z3	3	_____	3
8–11	Increase HR with resistance (R) or cadence/rpm to top of Z3	3	_____	3
11–14	(Rec) to bottom of Z2	2	_____	3
14–17	Increase HR to top of Z3; your choice of (R) or rpm, seated	3	_____	3
17–20	(Rec) to bottom of Z2	2	_____	3
20–23	Increase HR to the top of Z3; your choice of (R) or rpm, standing	3	_____	3
23–26	(Rec) to bottom of Z2	2	_____	3
26–29	Increase HR to top of Z3; alternate (R) and rpm, seated	3	_____	3
29–32	(Rec) to bottom of Z2	2	_____	3
32–35	Increase HR to top of Z3; alternate (R) and rpm, standing	3	_____	3
35–38	3 min. (rec) to bottom of Z2	2	_____	3
38–41	Increase HR to the top of Z3 with an all-out sprint at high rpm, seated	3	_____	3
41–45	Warm down to bottom of Z2 then Z1	2 1	_____	4

WORKOUT 11. THE ZIPPER

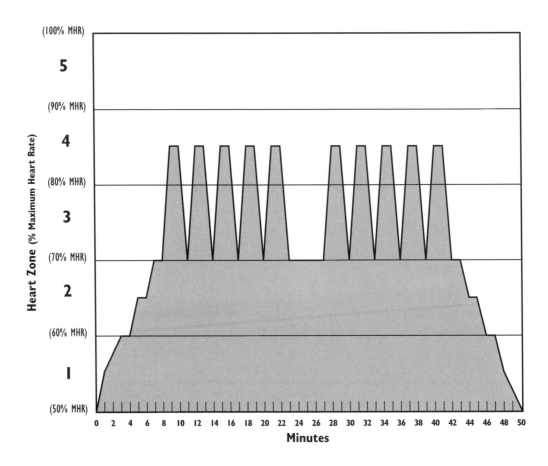

OVERVIEW

"Workout wonder" is what is about to happen to you. The primary wonder in this workout is to decide which hurts more, your legs burning or your lungs sucking air from the highest and hottest heart zones? Just like the teeth on a zipper, this ride might eat you up because it's close to a Red Line experience. For further wonders, crank up the sound of your Heart Zones Cycling Music Project[1] and join in with some fellow lactic acid–loving hedonists as you push yourself. Check out the workout profile and match its zipper shape with repeated high hot intervals.

DESCRIPTION

The purpose of the workout is lactic acid–tolerance training or developing your physiology to train through the high blood acidosis that results from anaerobic metabolism. By training at high heart rates, lactic acid concentrations build up in the specific muscles that are being worked and result in a sensation of "burn" in those muscles. Beware! Tomorrow you may be tired and sore—it's called *delayed muscle soreness*. You will also wonder why just a few intervals at a high intensity are so fatiguing. All lactic acid–tolerance training sessions stress you to near your max,

---

1. Check out the CD music that accompanies various workouts. Music composed to accompany workouts, called the Heart Zones Cycling Music Project, is available by visiting the www.heartzones.com web site.

and that's simply tough on the body. Nevertheless, your lactic acid tolerance will increase if you do this workout periodically, so enjoy zipping through this high, hot, and hard Heart Zones Cycling workout.

STATS AND TIPS FOR WORKOUT 11: THE ZIPPER

Zone Number and Name	Minutes in Zone	Heart Zone Training Points	Estimated Calories
5. Red Line			
4. Threshold	20	80	240–280
3. Aerobic	18	54	162–198
2. Temperate	8	16	48–64
1. Healthy Heart	4	4	12–20
Totals	50	154	462–562

Tip 1: If ten intervals are too hard in the beginning, start with five and build up to ten. Change body position frequently.

Tip 2: Increase intensity to 90% for a Red Line experience or performance training.

SEQUENCE FOR WORKOUT 11: THE ZIPPER

Elapsed Time (min.)	Workout Plan	Heart Zone	Your Heart Rate (bpm)	Riding Time (min.)
0–2	Warm up to bottom of Z1, easy pedal	1	_____	2
2–7	Warm up, easy pedal, steadily to midpoint of Z2	2	_____	5
7–9	Increase HR with cadence/rpm to bottom of Z3 (70%)	3	_____	2
9–24	First set: [Increase HR to midpoint of Z4 (85%) and sustain for 2 min. followed by 1 min. (rec) to bottom of Z3 (70%).] Repeat a total of 5 times, alternating standing and steated	4 3	_____	15
24–28	Easy pedal (rec) to the bottom of Z2 and sustain	2	_____	4
28–43	Second set: Repeat above work/recovery interval a total of 5 times. Change body position, cadence, and (R) each interval	4 3	_____	15
43–50	Warm down by gradually decreasing HR, easy pedal	2 2 1	_____ _____ _____	7

WORKOUT 12. A POSITIVE SPIN

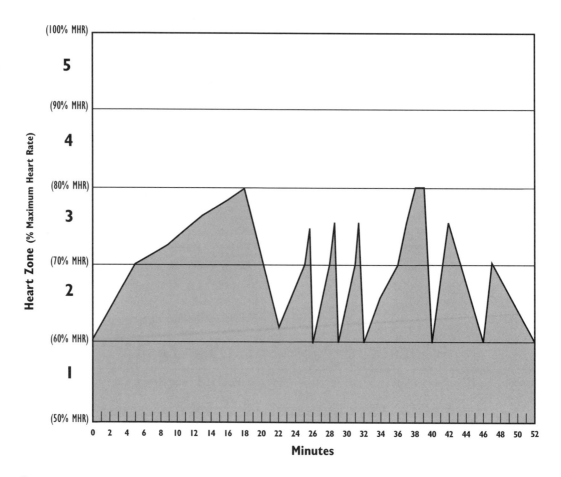

OVERVIEW

Approaching any workout—whether physical or mental—with a positive mental attitude and positive self-talk builds confidence. Confidence when connected with core values breeds a winning attitude that can lead to success. That's just what Positive Spin is guaranteed to provide for you—a workout on the pathway toward physical self-improvement.

STATS AND TIPS FOR WORKOUT 12: A POSITIVE SPIN

Zone Number and Name	Minutes in Zone	Heart Zone Training Points	Estimated Calories
5. Red Line			
4. Threshold	11	44	132–154
3. Aerobic	25	75	225–275
2. Temperate	16	32	96–128
1. Healthy Heart			
Totals	**52**	**151**	**453–557**

Tip: Feel the pressure against the top of your shoe when doing isolated-leg training.

DESCRIPTION

This workout provides the opportunity to visualize your goals and put on a "positive spin" with a positive "grin." Positive spin integrates the three components of strength, power, and leg speed by using interval training. The ride goals are to finish this workout with a grin and feel positive about your effort.

SEQUENCE FOR WORKOUT 12: A POSITIVE SPIN

Elapsed Time (min.)	Workout Plan	Heart Zone	Your Heart Rate (bpm)	Riding Time (min.)
0–5	Warm up to bottom of Z2	2	_____	5
5–10	Increase HR to bottom of Z3	3	_____	5
10–22	Pyramid climb[a] at 30–30 [30 sec. sprint–30 sec. (rec)], 60–30, 90–30, 120–30, 90–30, 60–30, 30–30. Keep HR in Z3 and Z4	3 3 4 4	_____ _____ _____ _____	12
22–25	(Rec) to bottom of Z2	2	_____	3
25–34	[A 3 min. interval broken down into a 30 sec. fast pedal to bottom Z3 followed by 30 sec. moderate to heavy (R) to midpoint of Z3 followed by a 2 min. (rec) to bottom of Z2.] Repeat a total of 3 times	3 2	_____ _____	9
34–42	From the bottom of Z2 add 10 bpm for 2 min. From midpoint of Z2 add 10 bpm, moderate (R) for 1 min. Add 10 bpm, fast spin for 1 min. Add 10 bpm, heavy (R), for 1 min. Sustain 80% standing for 1 more min. Finish with a 2 min. (rec) to bottom of Z2	2 2 3 4 4 2	_____ _____ _____ _____ _____ _____	8
42–46	Isolated-leg training[b] (ILT) 2 min. each leg, 60 rpm (6), heavy (R)	3	_____	4
46–47	Easy pedal both legs to bottom of Z2	2	_____	1
47–50	[Spin ups[c] from 60 rpm (6) to 140 rpm (14) in 1 min., increasing 10 rpm every 10 seconds.] Repeat a total of 3 times	3 2	_____ _____	3
50–52	Warm down to bottom of Z2	2	_____	2

[a] Incremental increases and decreases in time and intensity. Think of climbing up and then down a mountain. In this workout the work-interval durations increase and then decrease whereas the recover-interval duration stays at 30 seconds. The pattern is 30–30, 60–30, 90–30, and so on.

[b] Pedal with only one leg; rest the other on a box or stool. You may also rest it on the bike frame if you are riding a spin bike or simply keep your feet on the pedals and allow one leg to relax while the other does the work.

[c] Increase the cadence progressively by 5 to 10 rpm at regular intervals. Keep your legs under control. Concentrate on smooth pedaling and no bouncing.

WORKOUT 13. AFTERBURNER

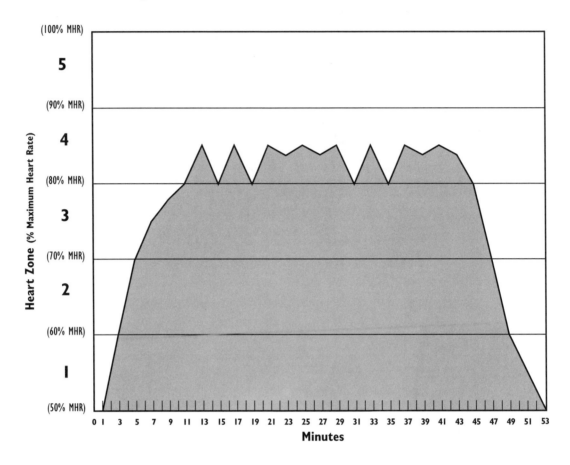

OVERVIEW

This workout is one big fat burner. The goal is to spend as much time at or just below your estimated anaerobic threshold heart rate in order to burn the most fat. Pick a heart rate number that you can train at (or just below) for an extended period of time.

DESCRIPTION

One of the best ways to maximize your fat-burning potential is to train near your "crossover point" and work to raise it. The crossover point, also known as your *anaerobic threshold heart rate*, is the point at which, if you cross over it to a higher heart rate, your body's cells will switch from aerobic to anaerobic metabolism, and you will not be burning any additional fat, just additional carbohydrates. However, the higher your anaerobic threshold number, the higher your "fat-burn rate."

This workout assumes your anaerobic threshold to be at about 85% of your maximum heart rate. Your individual crossover heart rate may be higher or lower than this percentage, depending on your fitness level.

STATS AND TIPS FOR WORKOUT 13: AFTERBURNER

Zone Number and Name	Minutes in Zone	Heart Zone Training Points	Estimated Calories
5. Red Line			
4. Threshold	36	144	432–504
3. Aerobic	8	24	72–88
2. Temperate	4	8	24–32
1. Healthy Heart	5	5	15–25
Totals	**53**	**181**	**543–649**

Tip: To lose 1 pound of body fat, you must burn approximately 3500 more calories than you eat.

SEQUENCE FOR WORKOUT 13: AFTERBURNER

Elapsed Time (min.)	Workout Plan	Heart Zone	Your Heart Rate (bpm)	Riding Time (min.)
0–5	Warm up to bottom of Z2 (60%)	2	_____	5
5–7	Increase HR to bottom of Z3 (70%)	3	_____	2
7–9	Increase HR 10 bpm, choice	3	_____	2
9–11	Increase HR 5 bpm, choice	3	_____	2
11–13	Increase HR bottom of Z4 (80%), choice	4	_____	2
13–21	[Increase HR 10 bpm or to AT for 2 min., choice, then decrease HR to bottom of Z4 for 2 min.] Repeat	4 / 4	_____ / _____	8
21–29	[From bottom of Z4 increase HR 10 bpm for 2 min., choice, then decrease HR 5 bpm for 2 min.] Repeat	4 / 4	_____ / _____	8
29–37	[Increase HR 5 bpm for 2 min., choice, then decrease HR to bottom of Z4 for 2 min.] Repeat	4 / 4	_____ / _____	8
37–45	[From bottom of Z4 increase HR 10 bpm for 2 min., choice, then decrease HR 5 bpm for 2 min]. Repeat	4 / 4	_____ / _____	8
45–47	Decrease HR to bottom of Z4	4	_____	2
47–49	Decrease HR to bottom of Z3	3	_____	2
49–51	Decrease HR to bottom of Z2	2	_____	2
51–53	Warm down	1	_____	2

Workout 14. Fast Lane!

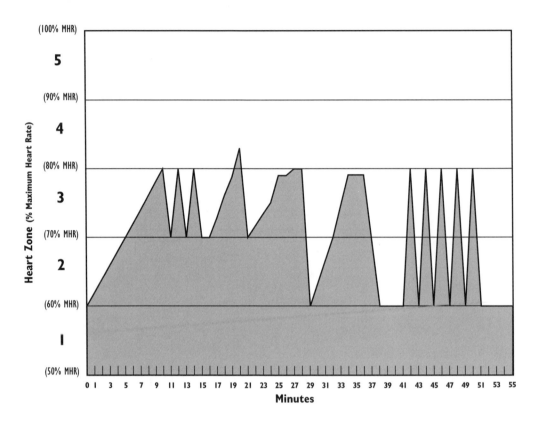

Overview

Life can be ridden in the "Fast Lane!" For most cyclists, this is the place to be. The fast lane is an expressway to getting faster and stronger as you look back just long enough to appreciate where you started.

Description

This workout is designed to enhance the functional capacity of the heart, lungs, and vascular system. You will push yourself through the Aerobic Zone and into the anaerobic Threshold Zone. Briefly, you will get a taste of training with less oxygen and with an increasing acidosis feeling from the lactic acid as it accumulates in your blood stream and in your cycling-specific muscles. Your time spent in Zone 3 will feel great because while riding in Zone 3, you get to release both emotionally and physically some of your stored-up toxins. Training in Zone 3 also builds resistance to fatigue and increases cardiovascular efficiency. Fast-lane riding also trains the metabolic pathways to spare carbohydrates and metabolize fatty acids. Some riders get addicted to riding in the fast lane, not just because it's fun but because of those wonderful, natural, mood-altering endorphins that are so profuse in Zone 3 and Zone 4.

STATS AND TIPS FOR WORKOUT 14: FAST LANE!

Zone Number and Name	Minutes in Zone	Heart Zone Training Points	Estimated Calories
5. Red Line			
4. Threshold	11	44	132–154
3. Aerobic	24	72	216–264
2. Temperate	20	40	120–160
1. Healthy Heart			
Totals	**55**	**156**	**468–578**

Tip: During hard pedaling, allow your foot to fall (float) without exerting force every three or four strokes. This helps delay muscle fatigue.

SEQUENCE FOR WORKOUT 14: FAST LANE!

Elapsed Time (min.)	Workout Plan	Heart Zone	Your Heart Rate (bpm)	Riding Time (min.)
0–10	Warm up gradually to bottom of Z2	2	_____	10
10–16	[From bottom of Z2 add approximately 30 bpm to midpoint of Z3 in 1 min., then (rec) to the bottom of Z2 in 1 min.] Repeat a total of 3 times	3 2	_____ _____	6
16–21	From the bottom of Z2 add 5 bpm each min. for 5 min. using (R) and 80 rpm (8)	3 4	_____ _____	5
21–24	(Rec) to the bottom of Z2	2	_____	3
24–29	5 min. interval—alternate 10 sec. "on"[a] and 10 sec. "off"[b]—standing and seated	3 4	_____ _____	5
29–32	(Rec) to the bottom of Z2	2	_____	3
32–38	[6 min. interval—30 sec. superspin[c] and 30 sec. easy pedal (rec).] Repeat a total of 6 times	3	_____	6
38–42	(Rec) to bottom of Z2	2	_____	4
42–52	[From bottom of Z2 increase HR to the bottom of Z4 in 1 min. all-out effort. (Rec) to Z2 in 1 min.] Repeat a total of 5 times	4 2	_____ _____	10
52–55	Gradually warm down to Z2 and Z1	2 1	_____ _____	3

Note: For a performance workout increase to 90%.

[a] Work interval (hard pedal) for specific amount of time.
[b] Recovery interval (easy pedal) for specific amount of time.
[c] Controlled pedaling or spinning above 120 rpm.

WORKOUT 15. FOOTLOOSE

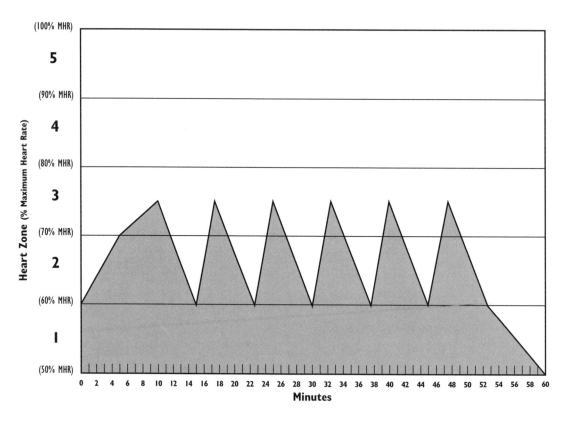

OVERVIEW

This ride will be a fun one for you. Just relax and stay loose! Use Footloose as a recovery ride, keeping the intensity low and the resistance off. This is what *active recovery* is all about, an easy time for your muscles and heart. Use this ride to measure your recovery heart rate or the number of beats you drop in a set amount of time.

DESCRIPTION

Ride for the entire workout between 60% and 75% of your maximum heart rate. This approach will allow your muscles and legs to remain active while giving your heart a rest from a recent high-intensity workout. Keep the resistance low and spin easy on your way up and down each interval.

To determine how quickly your heart recovers after exercise, measure how many seconds it takes for you to drop from 75% of your maximum heart rate down to 60%. Another approach tests recovery heart rate by seeing how many beats per minute your heart rate drops in 2 minutes with easy pedaling.

Either way, make sure your recovery cadence is the same on each recovery. Ride with little or no resistance (easy gearing) throughout this workout.

STATS AND TIPS FOR WORKOUT 15: FOOTLOOSE

Zone Number and Name	Minutes in Zone	Heart Zone Training Points	Estimated Calories
5. Red Line			
4. Threshold			
3. Aerobic	35	105	315–385
2. Temperate	20	40	120–160
1. Healthy Heart	5	5	15–25
Totals	**60**	**150**	**450–570**

Tip: As you get fitter, it takes less time to recover. Retest your recovery once a month.

SEQUENCE FOR WORKOUT 15: FOOTLOOSE

Elapsed Time (min.)	Workout Plan	Heart Zone	Your Heart Rate (bpm)	Riding Time (min.)
0–5	Warm up, easy pedal	2	_____	5
5–10	Steadily increase HR to bottom of Z3 (70%)	3	_____	5
10–15	Increase HR to midpoint of Z3 (75%) with steadily increasing rpm	3	_____	5
15–17.5	(Rec) to bottom of Z2 (60%)	2	_____	2.5
17.5–22.5	Increase HR to midpoint of Z3 (75%) with steadily increasing rpm	3	_____	5
22.5–25	Count number of recovery heartbeats in 2 min. You may go below Z2 (60%). Easy pedal	2	_____	2.5
25–30	Increase HR to midpoint of Z3 (75%) with steadily increasing rpm	3	_____	5
30–32.5	Count number of seconds it takes to (rec) to bottom of Z2 (60%). Easy pedal	2	_____	2.5
32.5–37.5	Increase HR to midpoint of Z3 (75%) with steadily increasing rpm.	3	_____	5
37.5–40	Count number of recovery heartbeats in 2 min. You may go below Z2 (60%). Easy pedal	2	_____	2.5
40–45	Increase HR to midpoint of Z3 (75%) with steadily increasing rpm	3	_____	5
45–47.5	Count number of seconds it takes to (rec) to bottom of Z2 (60%). Easy pedal	2	_____	2.5
47.5–52.5	Increase HR to midpoint of Z3 (75%) with fast cadence then sustain	3	_____	5
52.5–60	(Rec) to bottom of Z2 (60%) then Z1 (50%).	2 / 1	_____ _____	7.5

Note: Recovery may be timed and a new interval started once the bottom of Z2 is reached. Count the number of completed work/recovery intervals in 40 minutes.

WORKOUT 16. HEARTBEAT

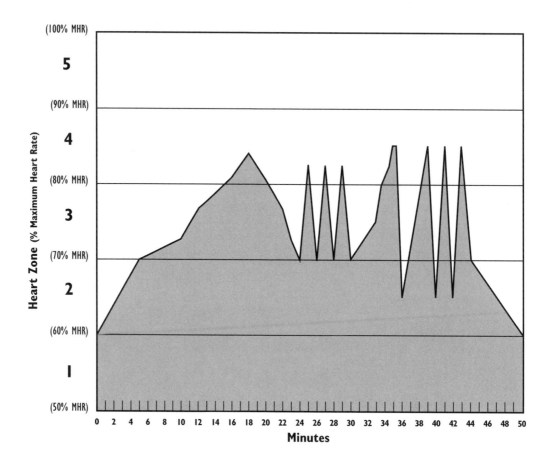

OVERVIEW

This workout gives you four different workout challenges. It starts with a Five by Two ladder. Next, you're challenged to finish a crisscross from the bottom to the top of Zone 3. Third, you ride yourself through a set of power and sprint intervals. Finally, you finish with a crisscross from the midpoint of Zone 2 to the midpoint of Zone 4.

DESCRIPTION

Each of these four challenges produces its own outcome. The Five by Two ladder simulates a long uphill pull that does nothing but get steeper. It also includes a controlled recovery back down the ladder that simulates a long downhill to give you some breathing time. A 2-minute, crisscross interval follows to train your aerobic system in Zone 3. The next interval pushes the heart rate higher as the heart and muscles are trained to respond quickly in 10-second sprints followed by 20-second recoveries. The last interval is a final push through two zones as you race against the clock. All in all, you'll feel you have trained for improved power and recovery from fatigue.

STATS AND TIPS FOR WORKOUT 16: HEARTBEAT

Zone Number and Name	Minutes in Zone	Heart Zone Training Points	Estimated Calories
5. Red Line			
4. Threshold	14	56	168—196
3. Aerobic	21	63	189—231
2. Temperate	15	30	90—120
1. Healthy Heart			
Totals	**50**	**149**	**447—547**

Tip: Use your monitor to test for improvements in your recovery heart rate.

SEQUENCE FOR WORKOUT 16: HEARTBEAT

Elapsed Time (min.)	Workout Plan	Heart Zone	Your Heart Rate (bpm)	Riding Time (min.)
0–5	Warm up to bottom of Z2	2	_____	5
5–10	Increase HR to bottom of Z3 with cadence/rpm	3	_____	5
10–20	From the bottom of Z3 add 5 bpm every 2 min., choice of (R) or (rpm), seated	3 / 4	_____ _____	10
20–25	Decrease HR 5 bpm every min. for 5 min. to bottom of Z3	4 / 3	_____ _____	5
25–33	[Increase HR from bottom of Z3 to bottom of Z4 in 1 min., your choice, followed by a 1 min. (rec) to bottom of Z3, count recovery beats (RHR).] Repeat 3 times with a final 2 min. (rec) at the bottom of Z3	3 / 4 / 3 / 4 / 3 / 4 / 3	_____ _____ _____ _____ _____ _____ _____	8
33–36	[Power starts[a] with heavy (R), standing for 10 sec. followed by 20 sec. seated (rec).] Repeat a total of 6 times	3 / 4 / 4 / 4 / 4	_____ _____ _____ _____ _____	3
36–39	Easy pedal (rec) to bottom of Z2	2	_____	3
39–45	Increase HR from midpoint of Z2 (65%) to midpoint of Z4 (85%) and (rec) to midpoint of Z2 (65%). Count number of times you complete this interval in 6 min.	2 / 4 / 2	_____ _____ _____	6
45–50	Warm down to bottom of Z2	2	_____	5

[a] From a slow spin or stopped position, seated or standing, expend in 10 seconds all-out effort with heavy resistance followed by a 20-second recovery. Alternate your lead foot.

WORKOUT 17. HOT ROD HEART

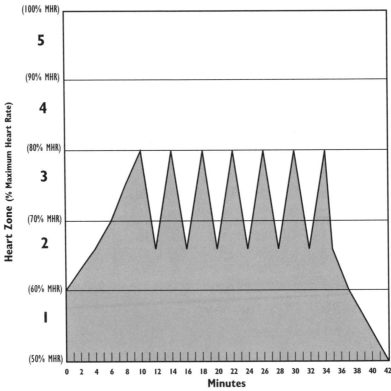

OVERVIEW

It is important to any cyclist to develop aerobic endurance. It is equally important to develop anaerobic endurance if you want to train to achieve performance goals. The difference between the two is one letter in the F.I.T. formula. In this formula that measures training load, the *F* stands for frequency or the number of workouts. The *I* stands for intensity or the heart zones that you

STATS AND TIPS FOR WORKOUT 17: HOT ROD HEART

Zone Number and Name	Minutes in Zone	Heart Zone Training Points	Estimated Calories
5. Red Line			
4. Threshold	14	56	168–196
3. Aerobic	4	12	36–44
2. Temperate	22	44	132–176
1. Healthy Heart	2	2	6–10
Totals	42	114	342–426

Tip 1: Alternate fast, seated, 30-bpm sprint intervals with slower, standing, 30-bpm heavy-resistance intervals.

Tip 2: "Aerobic endurance is the ability to continue the movement of a large amount of muscle mass for a long period of time" (Jenny Williams and Rae Nunan, *Heart Rate Fitness Program for Australia Schools* [Pursuit Performance, Australia, p. 12.]).

use. The *T* stands for time or riding duration. The one letter in the F.I.T. formula that distinguishes between aerobic and anaerobic endurance is the *I* for intensity. Heart rate monitors provide you with the data about how hard—that is, at what exercise intensity—you are riding. Depending on your heart rate number, you are riding either aerobically or anaerobically.

DESCRIPTION

This workout, Hot Rod Heart, gives you an opportunity to develop both aerobic and anaerobic endurance within a brief time frame. If your cardiovascular goal is to get fitter and you have been working out three or more times per week, choose this workout and bounce back and forth between work (riding in high heart zones) and recovery (riding in low heart zones) as you watch approximately a 30-bpm interval on your monitor. If it's your first time, it's quite a sight to see.

SEQUENCE FOR WORKOUT 17: HOT ROD HEART

Elapsed Time (min.)	Workout Plan	Heart Zone	Your Heart Rate (bpm)	Riding Time (min.)
0–4	Warm up to bottom of Z2, easy pedal	2	_____	4
4–6	Increase resistance (R) or rpm to midpoint of Z2 (65%)	2	_____	2
6–8	Increase HR to bottom Z3 (70%), your choice of (R), rpm, or combination	3	_____	2
8–10	Increase HR to midpoint of Z3	3	_____	2
10–12	Increase HR to bottom of Z4 (80%), heavy (R), standing	4	_____	2
12–14	(Rec) to midpoint of Z2 (65%)	2	_____	2
14–16	Increase HR approximately 30 bpm to bottom of Z4, seated sprint	4	_____	2
16–18	(Rec) to midpoint of Z2	2	_____	2
18–20	Increase HR approximately 30 bpm to bottom of Z4, heavy (R), standing	4	_____	2
20–22	(Rec) to midpoint of Z2	2	_____	2
22–24	Increase HR approximately 30 bpm to bottom of Z4, seated sprint	4	_____	2
24–26	(Rec) to midpoint of Z2	2	_____	2
26–28	Increase HR approximately 30 bpm to bottom of Z4, heavy (R), standing	4	_____	2
28–30	(Rec) to midpoint of Z2	2	_____	2
30–32	Increase HR approximately 30 bpm to bottom of Z4, seated, sprint	4	_____	2
32–34	(Rec) to midpoint of Z2	2	_____	2
34–36	Increase HR approximately 30 bpm to bottom of Z4, heavy (R), standing	4	_____	2
36–42	Warm down gradually to bottom of Z2 then to bottom of Z1	2 1	_____	6

WORKOUT 18. HOT SHOT

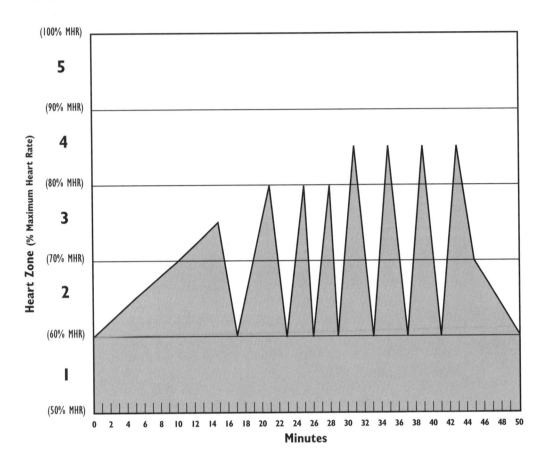

OVERVIEW

If you want to practice your acceleration skills with quick jumps, this could be a weekly workout ride for you. Imagine that you are staging a sneak attack around another cyclist each time you ride Hot Shot. This workout is a series of eight interval sprints that provide you with the tools to stay in front after you make that aggressive pass.

DESCRIPTION

Attack each of the work intervals with a quick, powerful jump, concentrating on reaching your heart rate goal as fast as possible and then sustaining that heart rate for the remainder of the time. You'll develop power, strength, and balance from these repeated jumps. Don't be surprised if you shoot over your heart rate goal at first. It takes experience to learn how your heart rate responds to quick changes in intensity. Precision heart rate training—Heart Zones Cycling—comes with that kind of experience.

STATS AND TIPS FOR WORKOUT 18: HOT SHOT

Zone Number and Name	Minutes in Zone	Heart Zone Training Points	Estimated Calories
5. Red Line			
4. Threshold	12	48	144–186
3. Aerobic	11	33	99–121
2. Temperate	27	54	162–216
1. Healthy Heart			
Totals	50	135	405–523

Tip: Accelerate out of the saddle until you can't spin any faster, then sit down and maintain the cadence until you reach your heart rate goal.

SEQUENCE FOR WORKOUT 18: HOT SHOT

Elapsed Time (min.)	Workout Plan	Heart Zone	Your Heart Rate (bpm)	Riding Time (min.)
0–5	Warm up to bottom of Z2 (60%), easy pedal	2	_____	5
5–10	Increase HR to midpoint of Z2 (65%), choice	2	_____	5
10–15	Increase HR to bottom of Z3 (70%), choice	3	_____	5
15–17	Increase HR to midpoint of Z3 (75%), choice	3	_____	2
17–19	(Rec) to bottom of Z2, easy pedal, drink water	2	_____	2
19–21	Increase HR to bottom of Z3, seated sprint	3	_____	2
21–23	Increase HR to bottom of Z4 (80%), standing sprint	4	_____	2
23–25	(Rec) to bottom of Z2, easy pedal	2	_____	2
25–26	Increase HR to bottom of Z4, standing sprint	4	_____	1
26–28	(Rec) to bottom of Z2, easy pedal	2	_____	2
28–29	Increase HR to bottom of Z4, standing sprint	4	_____	1
29–31	(Rec) to bottom of Z2, easy pedal, drink water	2	_____	2
31–47	[From bottom of Z2 increase HR to midpoint of Z4, (R) with a standing sprint for 2 min. followed by a 2 min. (rec) to bottom of Z2.] Repeat a total of 4 times	4 2	_____ _____	16
47–50	Warm down to bottom of Z2	2	_____	3

WORKOUT 19. KOOL HAND LUKE

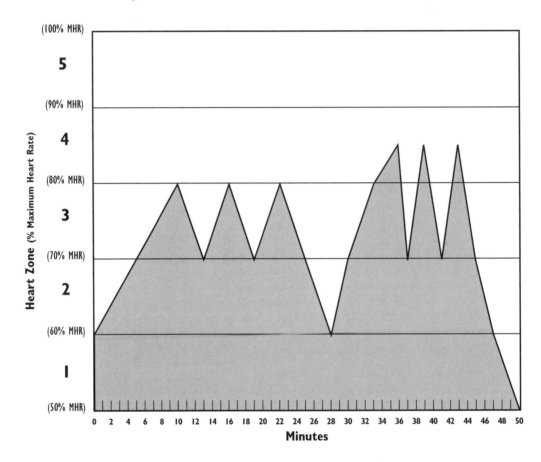

OVERVIEW

It takes a "kool hand" and a "kool head" to maneuver your way through this workout. The real test will be to keep a light "kool" touch on the handlebars while climbing hard and "hot" out of the saddle.

DESCRIPTION

In this workout, the cyclist goes through a series of six intervals while focusing on good climbing posture and strengthening the quads and hams. Stay "kool" by using all of the tricks in your hat to practice relaxation techniques on the bike. One way is to hold your upper body directly over the pedals as you change your hand positions. Slide back in the saddle for the seated climbs to develop more power, and as you stand, transfer your weight over the pedals from side to side, keeping the weight off the handlebars and using the power of your legs. Check your body

Drinking plenty of water is another way to stay "kool."

position in a mirror to make sure your weight is not too far forward over the front wheel. This workout is all about getting relaxed while you work hard and hot, so don't be afraid to crank up the resistance and climb. You can also raise your front wheel off the ground 3 to 5 inches to simulate a climbing position.

STATS AND TIPS FOR WORKOUT 19: KOOL HAND LUKE

Zone Number and Name	Minutes in Zone	Heart Zone Training Points	Estimated Calories
5. Red Line			
4. Threshold	17	68	204–238
3. Aerobic	23	69	207–253
2. Temperate	9	18	54–72
1. Healthy Heart	1	1	3–5
Totals	50	156	468–568

Tip: Stay "kool" by riding with your elbows gently bent and your arms and shoulders relaxed.

SEQUENCE FOR WORKOUT 19: KOOL HAND LUKE

Elapsed Time (min.)	Workout Plan	Heart Zone	Your Heart Rate (bpm)	Riding Time (min.)
0–5	Warm up to bottom of Z2, easy pedal	2	_____	5
5–10	Increase HR to bottom of Z3, choice	3	_____	5
10–28	[Gradually increase HR to bottom of Z4, heavy (R), seated, for 3 min., then decrease HR to bottom of Z3, easy pedal, for 3 min.] Repeat a total of 3 times	4 3	_____ _____	18
28–30	(Rec) to bottom of Z2, easy pedal. Drink water	2	_____	2
30–33	Increase HR to bottom of Z3, heavy (R), choice	3	_____	3
33–36	Increase HR to bottom of Z4, heavy (R), choice	4	_____	3
36–37	Increase HR to midpoint of Z4, heavy (R), standing	4	_____	1
37–39	Decrease HR to bottom of Z3, easy pedal	3	_____	2
39–47	[Increase HR to midpoint of Z4, heavy (R) standing, for 2 min., then decrease HR to bottom of Z3, easy pedal, for 2 min.] Repeat a total of 2 times	4 3	_____ _____	8
47–50	Warm down to bottom of Z2 then to bottom of Z1, easy pedal 2	2 1	_____ _____	3

WORKOUT 20. LADDER TO SUCCESS

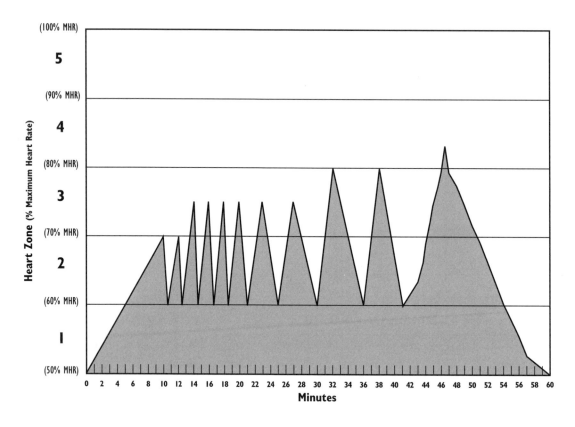

OVERVIEW

Most of us ride and train for our own, very personal, reasons. For some of us, exercise reduces stress, improves outlook, and gives us more energy. Identifying those reasons helps to keep us on the bike.

Here's a workout that can help you toward discovering that reason. While you are training on the bike, do some mental work and answer the question, "What's on those top few rungs of my ladder to success?" Revisit this ride and this question until you can verbalize a clear answer or statement that best answers the "why" question for you.

DESCRIPTION

This workout is a series of spin sprints, hill climbs, and a fast-paced pyramid climb into Zone 4 and back down, followed by a challenging, yet controlled recovery. The goal of this workout is to increase your leg speed and muscle power and train your body to adapt as workload increases. The 30-second interval sprints test how quickly you can raise your heart rate as well as how quickly you can recover. The heavy-resistance intervals simulate a series of five hills, each one steeper and longer. This pattern tests your muscular strength and endurance along with your mental toughness to hang in there. The pyramid climb develops your physiology to adapt to changes in power demands every 30 seconds. As a result, your cardiovascular system improves as you adapt to this progressive overload. The most challenging part for most riders is the 5 bpm decrease every minute. It takes skill to control your heart rate by only 5 bpm every minute. Coming back down the pyramid in a controlled manner makes for good contemplation time to answer the important and lifelong question about what success takes you toward.

STATS AND TIPS FOR WORKOUT 20: LADDER TO SUCCESS

Zone Number and Name	Minutes in Zone	Heart Zone Training Points	Estimated Calories
5. Red Line			
4. Threshold	7.5	30	90–105
3. Aerobic	14.5	43.5	130–160
2. Temperate	28	56	168–224
1. Healthy Heart	10	10	30–50
Totals	60	140	418–539

Tip: The first pedal stroke up the Ladder to Success is that of change. The first pedal stroke of change is learning.

SEQUENCE FOR WORKOUT 20: LADDER TO SUCCESS

Elapsed Time (min.)	Workout Plan	Heart Zone	Your Heart Rate (bpm)	Riding Time (min.)
0–5	Warm up to bottom of Z1, easy pedal	1	_____	5
5–10	Increase HR with rpm to bottom of Z2	2	_____	5
10–20	(5) 30 sec. sprints with 30 sec. (rec). Sprints start at the bottom of Z3 and go to the midpoint of Z3 (75%) then (rec) to bottom of Z2 (60%)	3 2	_____	10
20–32	[From bottom of Z2 increase HR with heavy (R) to midpoint of Z3 (75%) in 1 min. then (rec) to bottom of Z2 in 2 min.] Repeat a total of 4 times	3 2	_____	12
32–43	**Hill 1:** 4 min., standing, heavy (R), rpm above 60 (6) to bottom of Z4 then a 2 min. (rec) to bottom of Z2. **Hill 2:** 3 min., standing, heavy (R), rpm above 60 (6) to bottom of Z4 then a 2 min. (rec) to bottom of Z2.	4 2	_____	11
43–47	Pyramid climb[a] from the bottom of Z2 into Z4. Increase HR with (R) 5 bpm every 30 sec., steady tempo (cadence)	2 3 4	_____	4
47–60	From Z4 decrease HR 5 bpm every min. Mental focus! Controlled (rec)	4 3 2 1	_____	13

[a] Incremental increases and decreases in time and intensity. Think of climbing up a hill with a steady tempo or cadence and adding resistance or gearing to increase your heart rate. [For more information on pyramid climbing, read *More Energy, Less Stress* by Dan Rudd, Ph.D., and Sally Edwards (Heart Zone Publishing, 2001).]

WORKOUT 21. LANCELOT

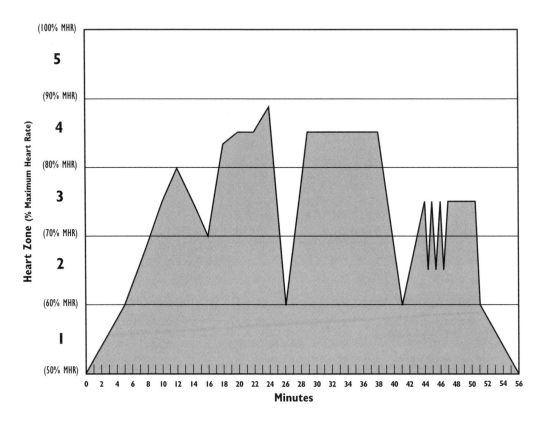

OVERVIEW

This workout is named after one America's greatest male cyclists, Lance Armstrong. His amazing comeback from cancer and his determination to beat the odds have provided inspiration for many people. Lance is "one in a million" physiologically, but we average folks can still take advantage of his training techniques to reach our own personal training goals.

STATS AND TIPS FOR WORKOUT 21: LANCELOT

Zone Number and Name	Minutes in Zone	Heart Zone Training Points	Estimated Calories
5. Red Line			
4. Threshold	22	88	264–308
3. Aerobic	11.5	34.5	103–126
2. Temperate	14.5	28.5	87–116
1. Healthy Heart	8	8	24–40
Totals	56	159	478–590

Tip: Training is individual and dependent on your genetics combined with your physiological capacity.

DESCRIPTION

There are four major goals in this ride. First, developing muscular strength and endurance with a low rpm and moderate to heavy resistance or gearing. Next, power starts from a standing position to practice that quick, powerful start or jump that Lance is an expert at. Third, learning to sustain faster bike speeds by training at your anaerobic threshold. Thus, pick the highest sustainable heart rate for a 12-minute period (the higher the percentage of maximum heart rate, typically the fitter you are). Fourth, training those neurological pathways with high-rpm speed work.

SEQUENCE FOR WORKOUT 21: LANCELOT

Elapsed Time (min.)	Workout Plan	Heart Zone	Your Heart Rate (bpm)	Riding Time (min.)
0–5	Warm-up in Z1	1	_____	5
5–10	Easy pedal to bottom of Z2	2	_____	5
10–16	Increase HR 10 bpm every 2 min. with (R), steady cadence/tempo, 50–60 rpm (5–6)	2 3 3	_____ _____ _____	6
16–18	Sustain HR at bottom of Z3	3	_____	2
18–26	[Standing power starts[a] with 10 sec. heavy (R) all-out effort sprint from a slow spin followed by a 20 sec. easy pedal (rec).] Repeat a total of 16 times	4	_____	8
26–29	Easy pedal (rec) to bottom of Z2	2	_____	3
29–41	Anaerobic threshold (AT) training[b] at highest sustainable HR	4	_____	12
41–44	Easy pedal (rec) to bottom of Z2	2	_____	3
44–47	[Spin ups[c] from 70 rpm (7) to 120 rpm (12) in 30 sec. with a 30 sec. easy pedal (rec).] Repeat a total of 3 times	2–3	_____	3
47–51	Spin ups with isolated leg training[d]: 30 sec. spin up with left leg, 30 sec. easy pedal (rec), then switch to right leg spin up 30 sec. with a 30 sec. easy pedal (Rec). Repeat a total of 4 times	3	_____	4
51–56	Warm down easy pedal to Z2 then Z1	2 1	_____ _____	5

[a] In a standing position and from a slow spin or roll, expend all-out effort for 10 seconds by using heavy resistance or hard gearing followed by 20 seconds of recovery or easy pedaling. Alternate lead foot.

[b] Riding at, about, or around your estimated anaerobic threshold. Typically this is the highest heart rate number you can sustain for an extended period of time.

[c] Increasing cadence or rpm 5 to 10 rpm at regular intervals while keeping the pedal stroke smooth and efficient.

[d] Pedaling with one leg at a time, resting the other on a box or stool, or simply keep your feet in the pedals and allow one leg to relax while the other leg does the work.

WORKOUT 22. PEEK-A-BOO

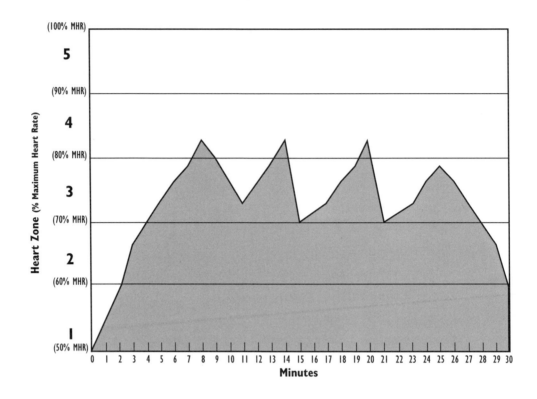

OVERVIEW

Like its name, this workout gives you a chance to "peek" into a higher zone. In addition, you'll get a taste of four heart zones although most of your workout time will be in Zone 3. Three times you take a "peek" at Zone 4, staying just a short time, and then you recover back down to the bottom of Zone 3.

DESCRIPTION

In cycling, you must constantly adapt to changing workloads that are thrown at you during the outdoor ride. Some of these changes are environmental and geographical such as hills, heat, altitude, and wind. This workout gives you constant exposure to changes that simulate those of weather, terrain, and other factors. The intensity changes almost every minute. The ride becomes more challenging as you near the top of Zone 3 and "peek" into Zone 4. Working out in these heart zones enhances functional capacity. Improvement in functional capacity comes from increases in the number and the size of blood vessels, an increase in vital capacity, and an increase in the size and strength of your heart.

STATS AND TIPS FOR WORKOUT 22: PEEK-A-BOO

Zone Number and Name	Minutes in Zone	Heart Zone Training Points	Estimated Calories
5. Red Line			
4. Threshold	2	8	24–28
3. Aerobic	22	66	198–242
2. Temperate	4	8	24–32
1. Healthy Heart	2	2	6–10
Totals	**30**	**84**	**252–312**

Tip: All things change when we do, especially our response to changes as a result of peaking at stress and then at recovery.

SEQUENCE FOR WORKOUT 22: PEEK-A-BOO

Elapsed Time (min.)	Workout Plan	Heart Zone	Your Heart Rate (bpm)	Riding Time (min.)
0–2	Warm up to top of Z1	1	_____	2
2–4	Easy pedal to midpoint of Z2 (65%)	2	_____	2
4–5	Increase HR to bottom of Z3 (70%) with cadence/rpm	3	_____	1
5–9	From the bottom of Z3, increase HR 5 bpm every min., choice	3 4	_____ _____	4
9–11	Timed (rec) to bottom of Z3, easy pedal, no (R). Count number of bpm dropped in 1 min.	3	_____	2
11–15	From the bottom of Z3, increase HR 5 bpm every min., (R), seated	3 4	_____ _____	4
15–17	Timed (rec) to bottom of Z3, easy pedal, no (R). Count number of bpm dropped in 1 min.	3	_____	2
17–21	From the bottom of Z3, increase HR 5 bpm every min. with cadence/rpm	3 4	_____ _____	4
21–23	Timed (rec) to bottom of Z3, easy pedal, no (R). Count number of bpm dropped in 1 min.	3	_____	2
23–26	From the bottom of Z3, increase HR 5 bpm each min. for 3 min., choice	3	_____	3
26–28	Decrease HR 5 bpm each min. for 2 min.	3	_____	2
28–30	Warm down to bottom of Z2, easy pedal	2	_____	2

WORKOUT 23. TAILWIND

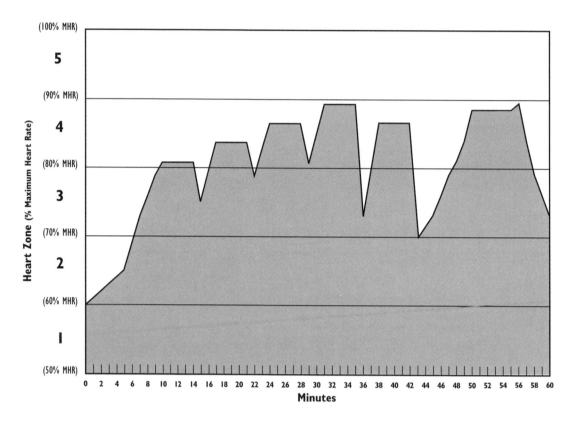

OVERVIEW

Tailwind is one of those words you love as a cyclist. Wind pushing you from your back—a tailwind—is a cyclist's dream. When air is pushing you from behind, it's like having the hand of God patting you and saying, "Good job."

DESCRIPTION

Tailwind is an interval workout, a combination of moderate- to high-intensity work followed by brief periods of recovery. More than half of your riding time is in Zone 4. Always be aware that when you spend a large part of your training time at or above your aerobic threshold metabolism, it's hard on your physiology. This session is loaded with challenges. Vary the work intervals by changing cadence, position on the bike, adding resistance, or changing gears. For example, you may want to "spin" your way up the first two thirds of the work interval using high cadence and low resistance or easy gearing and then add resistance or harder gearing to power your way up the last third. As you crest the hill or approach the end of the work interval, feel the relief as the tailwind again pushes at your back.

STATS AND TIPS FOR WORKOUT 23: TAILWIND

Zone Number and Name	Minutes in Zone	Heart Zone Training Points	Estimated Calories
5. Red Line			
4. Threshold	36	144	432–504
3. Aerobic	17	51	153–187
2. Temperate	7	14	42–56
1. Healthy Heart			
Totals	**60**	**209**	**627–747**

Tip: To develop a smooth, round, pedal stroke, envision your knee reaching up as if it were to touch the handlebar at the top of the stroke.

SEQUENCE FOR WORKOUT 23: TAILWIND

Elapsed Time (min.)	Workout Plan	Heart Zone	Your Heart Rate (bpm)	Riding Time (min.)
0–5	Warm up to bottom of Z2 (60%), easy pedal	2	_____	5
5–7	Add 10 bpm with cadence/rpm	2	_____	2
7–11	Add 5 bpm each min. for 4 min. with cadence/rpm	3	_____	4
11–15	Sustain HR at bottom of Z4 (80%), choice	4	_____	4
15–17	2 min. (rec) to midpoint of Z3 (75%)	3	_____	2
17–22	Increase HR to max. HR minus 30 bpm, sustain for 5 min., choice	4	_____	5
22–24	(Rec) to midpoint of Z3 (75%)	3	_____	2
24–29	Increase HR to midpoint Z4 (85%), sprint	4	_____	5
29–31	Decrease HR to bottom of Z4, 90 rpm (9)	4	_____	2
31–36	Increase HR to top of Z4 and sprint first 3 min. then heavy (R) last 2 min., 60 rpm (6), standing	4	_____	5
36–38	Decrease HR to max. HR minus 50 bpm	3	_____	2
38–43	Increase HR 25 bpm, choice	4	_____	5
43–45	(Rec) to bottom of Z3	3	_____	2
45–50	From bottom of Z3, increase HR 5 bpm each min. for 5 min.	3/4	_____	5
50–55	Increase HR 10 bpm and sustain, choice	4	_____	5
55–56	Increase HR to top of Z4, choice	4	_____	1
56–57	Decrease HR to bottom of Z4	4	_____	1
57–58	Decrease HR to bottom of Z3	3	_____	1
58–60	Warm down to bottom of Z2	2	_____	2

Chapter 6
Training in the Performance Heart Zones

Performance training is hard, high, hot training for those folks who want to get as fit as they possibly can. It's good for burning calories and for feeling great.

By riding well, eating well, resting well, and living well, you ultimately have a chance of reaching your ideal performance body composition—your ideal ratio of muscle and lean mass to body fat. To achieve this state requires fine-tuning your training and dietary regime. This is an individual pursuit and must be accomplished in your own way. There is no one system to attain optimum performance or optimum body composition. Thankfully, there is a tool for individualizing your training. You guessed it! It's the heart rate monitor.

One of the best ways to reach your ideal performance body composition is to learn from all available sources, including books, workout classes, and seminars and workshops (offered by Heart Zones). Experimenting with your dietary habits and gaining more experience with different ways of reaching your personal state of emotional harmony also help. Remember, in large part, emotions are as important to reaching and maintaining a lean, strong body as are any of the other components of healthy living.

The Benefits and Challenges of High-Intensity Training

Training an appropriate amount of time in the high heart rate zones will definitely improve your performance. And, interestingly, workouts in Zones 4 and 5, while a challenge, can be some of your most enjoyable riding experiences. The reason is because it is in these zones that you really feel the effects of the "rider's high." When pushed to its limit, your body releases natural hormones known as endorphins that make you feel an incredible sense of well being and euphoria.

However, there is a down side. Ironically, riding too much in the Threshold and Red Line

Zones can decrease your performance. Spending all of your training time in the performance zones can result in injury, staleness, and a decrease in conditioning. The key is to have an individual riding dosage that is appropriate for your fitness level and closely matches an individual goal-based training plan. The true challenge for the performance-oriented rider is to reach the optimum amount of *training load*. Specifically, training load is the sum of the intensity, the frequency, and the amount of time (or duration) that you spend on the saddle. When your riding dosage and training plan synchronize, you can reach your highest fitness and performance levels.

The Rest of the Top Twenty Heart Zone Training Rules

If you have been Heart Zones Cycling for a while and have yet to see positive performance results, you may be overtraining by spending too much time in the upper heart zones. Or, you might not be spending enough time in those zones and are under-training. Remember those fourteen rules for heart zone training in chapter 4? Well, these last additional rules should help improve your performance. Let's pick up where we left off, with a few more details about the At-About-Around Threshold Rule:

❤ **The At-About-Around Rule:** If you recall from chapter 4, this rule states that you must train at-about-or-around your anaerobic threshold heart rate to get faster. If you spend too much time training above it, you will over-train, and if you spend too much time below it, you will stay fit but not get fitter. And, if you spend too much time above it, you will burn out and actually lower or suppress your anaerobic threshold heart rate.

The only accurate way to measure anaerobic threshold heart rate is to have a sports science lab, hospital, or other professional facility test you by using oxygen or lactate measurement methods. It's impossible to measure anaerobic threshold heart rate accurately on your own. However, there is one test that will give you a "guesstimate"—the *anaerobic threshold test*.

During your favorite sports activity, go as hard as you steadily can for 20 minutes. Record your average heart rate for that time, then rest for 5 minutes. Go for another highest and hardest 20 minutes and again record your average heart rate. The average heart rate of both 20-minute periods is close to your anaerobic threshold heart rate. This is a very strenuous workout, so be prepared to feel tired afterwards. Only take this test if you are in good shape and are comfortable exercising hard for 40 minutes. You can also estimate your anaerobic threshold heart rate by using a number that is slightly less (5–10 bpm) than your average heart rate during an all-out effort of 30 minutes riding as hard as you can sustain.

❤ **The 50% Rule:** This rule states that no more than 50% of the week's overall total training time should be spent in the performance zones. Too much time in the performance zones leads quickly to overtraining. For the high-performance endurance athlete who knows the importance of long intervals at high sustainable heart rates, it's easy to train too hard and too long. By using your heart rates and recording the time you spend in those zones, you can measure your performance zone training and back off for safety.

17 *The 24-Hour Rule:* The 24-Hour Rule states that you can do one performance zone (Zone 4 or 5) workout every 24 hours as long as you change disciplines. So, if you want to swim in the Red Line Zone one day, bike in the Red Line Zone the next day, and cross-country ski in the Red Line Zone the day after that, you can. Changing sports and, preferably, muscle groups allows the muscles specific to each sport to rest and recover before the next high-intensity zone workout.

18 *The 48-Hour Rule:* This rule states that you must wait 48 hours before doing another performance zone workout in the same sport. If you ride in the Red Line Zone on Monday, it's okay to ride in the Threshold Zone on Wednesday, provided that you rest on Tuesday. During the 48 hours of rest, the specific muscles that were used are allowed sufficient time for the recovery process to occur. It takes the body at least 48 hours to replenish the fuel stores necessary to have another performance zone workout.

19 *The Recovery Rule:* One of the most important measurements to take with your monitor is your recovery heart rate. The recovery heart rate is one of the best indicators of fitness. The longer it takes for your heart rate to recover, the greater the amount of your body's fatigue. If your heart rate does not recover sufficiently, it may indicate that you are overtraining or are experiencing the effects of other types of stress on your body. And, as your recovery times shorten, it's an indication that you are getting fitter.

There are a variety of recovery heart rate tests, but one of the most popular is the *"120-second" test.* The purpose of this test is to measure how well your heart returns to its ambient heart rate—that is, how well it is able to recover from the stresses of exercise. The faster your heart recovers, the better. If your heart rate returns to a number close to your ambient heart rate in this 2 minutes of recovery time, that's great. If not, you can at least determine how much your heart rate has dropped or decreased over the course of 2 minutes and compare that figure on a regular basis.

For example, if Sally Edwards is training in her Aerobic Zone at 150 bpm, 2 minutes after she completes her workout, she'll note her heart rate. If at the end of those 2 minutes, her heart rate has gone down to 90 bpm, her recovery heart rate will be 60 bpm, the difference between 150 bpm and 90 bpm. If Sally's recovery heart rates is generally about 60 bpm, and then one day she only sees a recovery heart rate of about 35 bpm, something is probably amiss and she should adjust her training plan and take it a little easy for a while.

20 *The Maximum Sustainable Heart Rate Rule:* The highest sustainable heart rate you can maintain over the longest period of time determines the fastest finishing time you can have in a competitive event. This is the heart rate to train in and get to know well, because it is that borderline heart rate that could take you either to success or blowout. For races longer than 20 minutes, this heart rate is probably below your anaerobic threshold, depending on environmental factors and your fitness level.

By using your heart rate monitor and following these basic rules, you should begin to see what we call "improvement effect HR," a measurement that shows changes in fitness. You will be able to train harder but at a lower HR than when you first began, providing proof that your training has been successful—you are fitter, stronger, and faster.

Go!

We call Zones 4 and 5 the high, hot, and hard ones because that's just what you're going to experience. Here are a few reminders to help keep these workouts enjoyable:

- Drink lots of water—staying properly hydrated makes the workout more comfortable and keeps your heart rate lower because it replaces the water in your blood that you lose through sweat
- Adequately warm up, especially for these strenuous rides where you are going to be applying a lot of force on your tendons, bones, and ligaments
- Focus on your breathing to help sustain the peak heart rate numbers you will hit

As athletes, we love Threshold and Red Line workouts, which is why we included so many of them in this workout book. But don't let the love of riding hard interfere with the intelligence of riding smart. You have "two hearts" in that big chest of yours—the emotional heart and the physical heart. Taking care of both is the true genius of high performance training. When you do, that's when you'll get the results you seek and lose body fat, decrease your stress, attain your fittness goals, and most of all, love your bike the most. Training smart leads to a smart heart.

WORKOUT 24. "10"

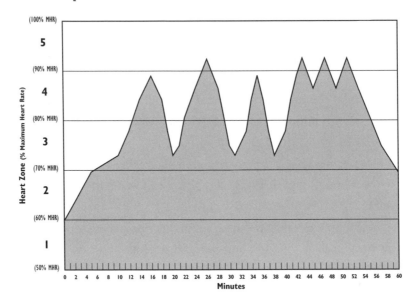

OVERVIEW

A "10" is a perfect score in some sports like gymnastics. This workout may feel like a "10" as you cavort on your balance beam—hmmm, ride your bike—but not because it is the perfect workout. Rather, it's a near-perfect 10 because it's at the top of the training-intensity range near that maximum heart rate number. You earn a lot more heart zone training points and burn a lot more calories when you ride the "10" compared to other workouts because it's nestled in the red-hot Zone 5.

DESCRIPTION

The workout named "10" was designed to be both physically demanding and also fun with a dose of mental challenges. Keep close track of your heart rate and stay on task. Mentally focus on your heart rate numbers because it takes that to keep them in the Red Line Zone. Reach into your magic hat of ways to increase and decrease the intensity and use all of them. The more often you do this workout, the easier it will be and the better you'll be at it.

STATS AND TIPS FOR WORKOUT 24: "10"

Zone Number and Name	Minutes in Zone	Heart Zone Training Points	Estimated Calories
5. Red Line	8	40	120–160
4. Threshold	25	100	300–350
3. Aerobic	21	63	189–231
2. Temperate	6	12	36–48
1. Healthy Heart			
Totals	**60**	**215**	**645–789**

Tip: Relaxing your shoulders helps keep your upper body free of tension.

SEQUENCE FOR WORKOUT 24: "10"

Elapsed Time (min.)	Workout Plan	Heart Zone	Your Heart Rate (bpm)	Riding Time (min.)
0–5	Warm up to bottom of Z2 (60%), easy pedal	2	_____	5
5–10	Increase HR to bottom of Z3 (70%), choice	3	_____	5
10–12	Increase HR to max. HR minus 50 bpm	3	_____	2
12–18	From max. HR minus 50 bpm, increase HR 10 beats every 2 min.	3 4 4	_____ _____ _____	6
18–21	Decrease HR 10 beats every min.	4 3 3	_____ _____ _____	3
21–22	Sustain HR at midpoint of Z3 (75%)	3	_____	1
22–26	Increase HR 10 bpm every 2 min.	4 4	_____ _____	4
26–28	Increase HR 5 bpm, choice	5	_____	2
28–31	Decrease HR 10 bpm every min.	4 4 3	_____ _____ _____	3
31–33	Decrease HR 5 bpm and sustain for 2 min.	3	_____	2
33–36	Increase HR 10 bpm every min.	3 4 4	_____ _____	3
36–38	Decrease HR 10 bpm every min.	4 3	_____	2
38–40	Decrease HR 10 bpm and sustain for 2 min.	3	_____	2
40–43	Increase HR 10 bpm every minute	3 4 4	_____ _____ _____	3
43–45	Increase HR 5 bpm, choice	5	_____	2
45–53	[Decrease HR 10 bpm for 2 min., then increase HR 10 bpm for 2 min.] Repeat interval a total of 2 times	4 5	_____ _____	8
53–55	Decrease HR 10 beats	4	_____	2
55–60	Warm down to bottom of Z2, easy pedal	2	_____	5

WORKOUT 25. FIVE BY FIVE

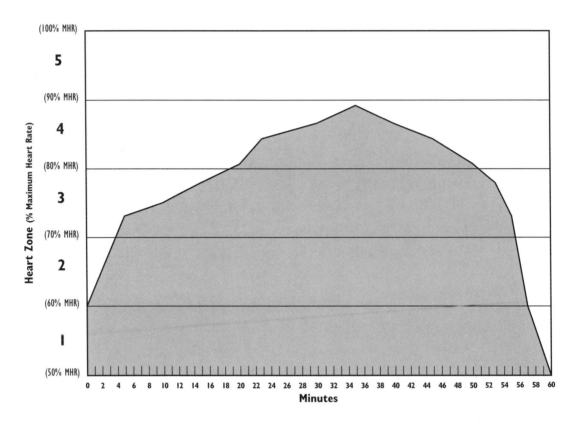

OVERVIEW

What does Harry Potter (the main character in the popular book *Harry Potter and the Sorcerer's Stone,* by J. K. Rowling [Random House, 1999]) and his Nimbus 2000 broomstick have in common with us ordinary muggles who love cycling? We both like riding high-performance, quick-responding machines that leave others in the dust. There is nothing like knowing your bike and your fitness level can work together as a fine-tuned machine, taking you to places only limited by your imagination. Whether your goal is being the star "seeker" on the Quidditch team at Hogwarts School of Witchcraft and Wizardry or the "yellow jersey" leader at the Tour de France, succeeding in the Five by Five workout scores big points for magical training.

DESCRIPTION

Think of this workout as a magical climb up a ladder. Each rung magically leads you further up into the stratosphere of intensity and physiology. Finally you reach the top and then travel gently back down to earth again.

Climbing up and over the magical ladder teaches your cycling-specific metabolic systems to adapt to changing workloads every so many minutes and forces your cardiovascular system to get stronger by adapting to the progressively increasing workload. Reaching the top is only half the battle; coming down in a controlled manner is even more challenging.

After warming up, start your adventure 50 bpm below your maximum heart rate. Gradually increase the intensity until you hover at the top where your heart rate is approximately 20 bpm below your maximum heart rate. After feeling the magic, descend gracefully back down.

STATS AND TIPS FOR WORKOUT 25: FIVE BY FIVE

Zone Number and Name	Minutes in Zone	Heart Zone Training Points	Estimated Calories
5. Red Line	5	25	70–100
4. Threshold	30	120	360–420
3. Aerobic	17	51	153–187
2. Temperate	7	14	42–56
1. Healthy Heart	1	1	3–5
Totals	60	211	628–768

Tip: Slide forward on the saddle—or broomstick!—to work the quadriceps and slide back on the saddle to work the glutes and hamstrings.

SEQUENCE FOR WORKOUT 25: FIVE BY FIVE

Elapsed Time (min.)	Workout Plan	Heart Zone	Your Heart Rate (bpm)	Riding Time (min.)
0–5	Warm up to bottom of Z2, easy pedal	2	_____	5
5–10	Increase HR to max. HR—50 bpm (bottom rung of the ladder)	3	_____	5
10–15	From max. HR minus 50 bpm, increase HR 5 bpm, choice	3	_____	5
15–20	Increase HR 5 bpm, choice	3	_____	5
20–25	Increase HR 5 bpm, choice	4	_____	5
25–30	Increase HR 5 bpm, choice	4	_____	5
30–35	Increase HR 5 bpm, choice	4	_____	5
35–40	Increase HR 5 bpm, choice	5	_____	5
40–45	Decrease HR 5 bpm, choice (be careful to only decrease 5 bpm in a controlled recovery)	4	_____	5
45–50	Decrease HR 5 bpm, choice	4	_____	5
50–53	Decrease HR 5 bpm, choice	4	_____	3
53–55	Decrease HR 5 bpm, choice	3	_____	2
55–57	Decrease HR 10 bpm, choice	3	_____	2
57–59	Decrease HR to bottom of Z2	2	_____	2
59–60	Warm down to bottom of Z1	1	_____	1

WORKOUT 26. AT, ABOUT, AND AROUND

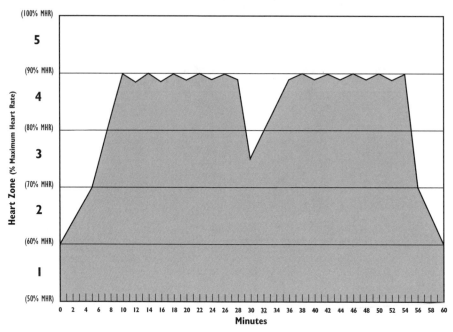

OVERVIEW

There are a number of complex concepts in cycle training. And there are several that are so important that they deserve a clearer understanding. At, About, and Around is a ride that teaches literally one of the more difficult training principles. In just one attempt at this ride, we guarantee that you will fully understand that this is probably the most challenging and mentally tough workout of the fifty that are catalogued here.

There is a training mechanism that occurs in the body when you work out near your individual and day-specific anaerobic threshold (or crossover) heart rate. When you train above your anaerobic threshold, there is not enough oxygen to sustain your effort for long. When you train At, About, and Around this heart rate number, you are at the threshold of burning the maximum amount of fat as well as at a point where training for long periods of time is not possible. The workout occurs "at" your specific anaerobic threshold heart rate number, "about" or close to that threshold heart rate number, and "around" or near that threshold heart rate number.

DESCRIPTION

As you improve your fitness, your training heart rate drops because you can do more exercise at a lower heart rate. Your anaerobic threshold heart rate goes up, however, as more exercise stress is required to reach your anaerobic threshold. *This is the very definition of fitness: to move your anaerobic threshold as close as you can to your maximum heart rate.* One of the best ways to improve your fitness and simultaneously raise your anaerobic threshold is to train at, about, and around that heart rate number. Choose a heart rate number that you think you can train at, about, and around for approximately 45 minutes. Heads up! This is one tough training ride.

To measure anaerobic threshold heart rate precisely, you must complete an exercise stress test in a laboratory setting where scientists measure your oxygen capacity—the amount of oxygen utilized—or by collecting blood samples to measure the lactic acid concentrations. Alternatively, you can estimate your anaerobic threshold heart rate by riding the At, About, and Around workout. Your highest sustainable heart rate number for this ride will be within 5 bpm of your true and laboratory-tested anaerobic threshold heart rate.

STATS AND TIPS FOR WORKOUT 26: AT, ABOUT, AND AROUND

Zone Number and Name	Minutes in Zone	Heart Zone Training Points	Estimated Calories
5. Red Line	20	100	300–400
4. Threshold	20	80	240–280
3. Aerobic	13	39	117–143
2. Temperate	7	14	42–56
1. Healthy Heart			
Totals	**60**	**233**	**699–879**

Tip: Your anaerobic threshold heart rate changes depending on your current level of fitness. Adjust your ride accordingly.

SEQUENCE FOR WORKOUT 26: AT, ABOUT, AND AROUND

Elapsed Time (min.)	Workout Plan	Heart Zone	Your Heart Rate (bpm)	Riding Time (min.)
0–5	Warm up to bottom of Z2 (60%)	2	_____	5
5–10	[Increase HR to bottom of Z3 (70%)	3	_____	5
10–12	Increase HR to AT estimate plus 5 bpm	5	_____	2
12–14	Decrease HR 5 bpm to AT	4	_____	2
14–16	Increase HR 5 bpm	5	_____	2
16–18	Decrease HR 5 bpm	4	_____	2
18–20	Increase HR 5 bpm	5	_____	2
20–22	Decrease HR 5 bpm	4	_____	2
22–24	Increase HR 5 bpm	5	_____	2
24–26	Decrease HR 5 bpm	4	_____	2
26–28	Increase HR 5 bpm	5	_____	2
28–30	Decrease HR 5 bpm	4	_____	2
30–36	Decrease HR to midpoint of Z3 (75%), easy pedal]	3	_____	6
36–56	Repeat minutes 10–30			20
56–58	Decrease HR to bottom of Z3 (70%)	3	_____	2
58–60	Warm down to bottom of Z2 (60%), easy pedal	2	_____	2

Note: Anaerobic threshold for a sedentary individual is often between 60% and 70% of their maximum heart rate. A fit individual's anaerobic threshold is often between 70% and 85%, and a super-fit individual is often between 85% and 95% of their maximum heart rate. For more information, refer to the anaerobic threshold chart in chapter 2.

WORKOUT 27. BLAZING SADDLES

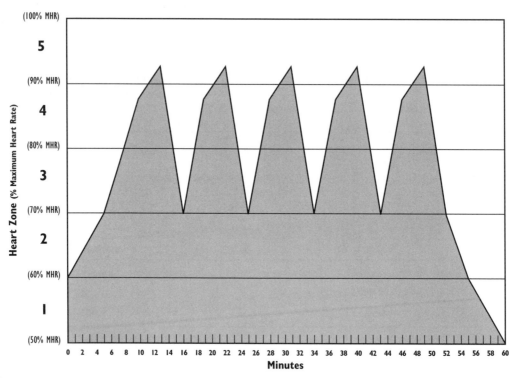

OVERVIEW

Lyle Nelson, a four-time American Olympic biathlete and captain of the United States' winter Olympic team, claims this as one of his favorite workouts. He used the Blazing Saddle format of repeating intervals of increases and decreases of 40 bpm to train, becoming one of the United States' most successful cross-country ski racers. Like most high-caliber athletes, Lyle always trained with his best friend, his heart rate monitor.

DESCRIPTION

Completing this 40-bpm interval workout with an Olympic-style smile is a challenge. This one is pure, hard intervals that will take you out of the comfort zone. Measure the elapsed time it takes for your heart rate to recover to the bottom of Zone 3, that is, to 70% of your maximum heart rate.

This is a workout to put your interval timer to work. Some monitors even capture the length of time it takes for you to reach your recovery heart rate. Still other models of heart rate monitors sound an audible alarm to announce you have reached that number. There are good web sites that provide you with details on interval heart rate monitors and their features. Don't wait until you have saved up the resources to acquire an interval monitor in order to do this workout. A basic heart rate monitor with time of day or stopwatch function will provide you with the numbers needed for recovery heart rate and interval training.

STATS AND TIPS FOR WORKOUT 27: BLAZING SADDLES

Zone Number and Name	Minutes in Zone	Heart Zone Training Points	Estimated Calories
5. Red Line	15	75	225–300
4. Threshold	15	60	180–210
3. Aerobic	20	60	180–220
2. Temperate	7	14	42–56
1. Healthy Heart	3	3	9–15
Totals	**60**	**212**	**636–801**

Tip 1: Resting or waking heart rate is a good indicator of training readiness. If you are overtraining, it is common to experience increases in your resting heart rate of 5 bpm above normal.

Tip 2: If your morning or waking heart rate is high, either drop down one or two heart zones for the day's training or take a day of complete rest.

SEQUENCE FOR WORKOUT 27: BLAZING SADDLES

Elapsed Time (min.)	Workout Plan	Heart Zone	Your Heart Rate (bpm)	Riding Time (min.)
0–5	Warm up to bottom of Z2, easy pedal	2	_____	5
5–10	Increase HR gradually to the bottom of Z3	3	_____	5
10–13	[Increase HR 30 bpm in 3 min., choice	4	_____	3
13–16	Increase HR gradually 10 bpm in 3 min., choice	5	_____	3
16–19	(Rec) to bottom of Z3]	3	_____	3
19–55	Repeat minutes 10–19 a total of 4 times			36
55–60	Warm down into Z2 then Z1	2	_____	5
		1	_____	

WORKOUT 28. BRAVEHEART

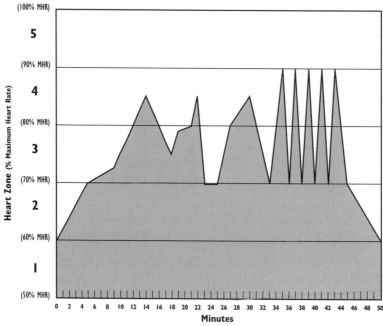

OVERVIEW

Hot, high, and hard training rides like this one are only ridden by those who like the gusto that comes with a courageous heart. Before you start your ride, act like the bravehearts of Scottish descendents and plan Celtic music for the full flair of the ride. Braveheart, like most Scottish dances and rides, is full of the spice of life—a variety of sprints, spin ups, power surges, isolated-leg training, and two-zone intervals.

DESCRIPTION

This 50-minute ride feels much harder than is reflected by its heart zone training points. Experience the challenging combination of strength-interval and sprint-interval work with little to no

STATS AND TIPS FOR WORKOUT 28: BRAVEHEART

Zone Number and Name	Minutes in Zone	Heart Zone Training Points	Estimated Calories
5. Red Line	5	25	75–100
4. Threshold	13	52	156–182
3. Aerobic	24	72	216–264
2. Temperate	8	16	48–64
1. Healthy Heart			
Totals	50	165	495–610

Tip: One heart zone training point is equal to 1 minute in a given zone multiplied by the zone number. To calculate the total number of heart zone training points for each zone, multiply the zone number by the number of minutes that you train in that zone and sum the results for the five zones.

steady-state riding. The recoveries are short and high—around 70% of your maximum heart rate. Reach for those last five heartbeats as you cross the finish line at 90% of your maximum heart rate.

SEQUENCE FOR WORKOUT 28: BRAVEHEART

Elapsed Time (min.)	Workout Plan	Heart Zone	Your Heart Rate (bpm)	Riding Time (min.)
0–5	Warm up to bottom of Z2, easy pedal	2	_____	5
5–9	Isolated-leg training[a] (ILT): Moderate to heavy (R), 60 rpm (6), 1 min. or each leg for a total of 4 min.	3	_____	4
9–15	From bottom of Z3, increase HR 5 bpm every min. for a total of 6 min.	3 3 3 4 4 4	_____ _____ _____ _____ _____ _____	6
15–19	Decrease HR 5 bpm every min. for 4 min.	4 4 4 3	_____ _____ _____ _____	4
19–23	[Power starts:[b] Moderate to heavy (R), 10 sec. hard effort, 10 sec. easy pedal.] Repeat a total of 12 times or 4 min.	3 4 4 4	_____ _____ _____ _____	4
23–25	(Rec) to bottom of Z3	3	_____	2
25–27	Spin ups:[c] From 60 rpm (6) add 10 rpm every 10 sec. to 120 rpm (12) and then decrease 10 rpm every 10 sec. to 60 rpm	3	_____	2
27–33	[Surges:[d] Moderate to heavy (R) for 30 sec., increase cadence for 30 sec.] Repeat this 1 min. interval a total of 6 times	4	_____	6
33–35	Easy pedal, (rec) to bottom of Z3	3	_____	2
35–45	Ups and downs:[e] Count the number of times for 10 min. from the bottom of Z3 to the bottom of Z5	3 5	_____ _____	10
45–50	Warm down to bottom of Z2, easy pedal	2	_____	5

[a] Pedal with only one leg, resting the other on a box or stool, or simply keep your feet in the pedals and allow one leg to relax while the other does the work.
[b] From a slow spin or stopped position, seated or standing, expend 10 seconds of all-out effort with heavy resistance followed by 10 seconds of easy pedaling or recovery. Alternate lead foot.
[c] Moderate to heavy resistance with cadence changes.
[d] Increase cadence progressively by 5 to 10 rpm at regular intervals, keeping the pedal stroke smooth and efficient.
[e] Count the number of times you increase heart rate and recover in a set period of time.

WORKOUT 29. CUTTING EDGE

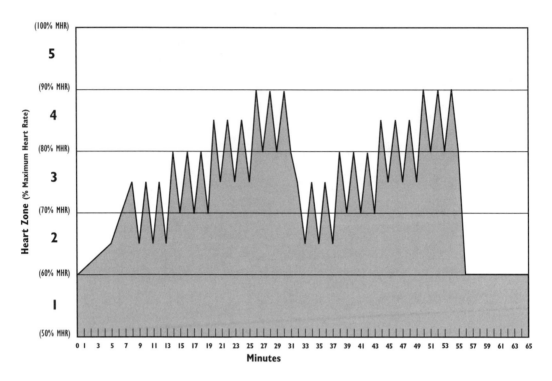

OVERVIEW

High tech and high touch are two of the trends in the new millennium. This workout combines both high tech and high touch as you ride with a high-tech heart rate monitor that uses ASICs (application-specific integrated circuits) to interpret the electrical impulse from the heart and then delivers the data to a wrist monitor. When you then use your mind to interpret the data, your mind touches your heart. Using a monitor provides you with the cutting-edge tool that serves as a window into your heart. This cutting-edge training allows you to leverage the power of technology with feeling.

STATS AND TIPS FOR WORKOUT 29: CUTTING EDGE

Zone Number and Name	Minutes in Zone	Heart Zone Training Points	Estimated Calories
5. Red Line	6	30	90–120
4. Threshold	18	72	216–252
3. Aerobic	18	54	162–198
2. Temperate	23	46	138–184
1. Healthy Heart			
Totals	**65**	**202**	**606–754**

Tip: Dont' waste your power by rocking from side to side on the bike saddle. Keep your rear end, head, hips, and arms aligned.

DESCRIPTION

The ride starts out easy and gets tough, so don't be fooled into thinking this is an easy workout. One look at the workout profile and you remember that the graph tells it all in one quick glance. This is a tough workout. The first half of the workout uses high rpm/cadence numbers to take you gradually toward higher heart rate numbers with brief respites of rest. The high-resistance or hard-gearing second half of the workout concentrates on building muscular strength and power as you reach high heart rate numbers. Each 30-minute segment uses the same heart rate intensities but uses two very different physiological ways to get you there.

SEQUENCE FOR WORKOUT 29: CUTTING EDGE

Elapsed Time (min.)	Workout Plan	Heart Zone	Your Heart Rate (bpm)	Riding Time (min.)
0–8	Warm up to midpoint of Z2 (65%), easy pedal	2	_____	8
8–14	[Increase HR to midpoint of Z3 (75%) for 1 min., 110 rpm (11), (R) as needed. (Rec) to midpoint of Z2 for 1 min.] Repeat a total of 3 times	2 3	_____ _____	6
14–20	[Increase HR from midpoint of Z2 to bottom of Z4 for 1 min., rpm 110 (11), (R) as needed. (Rec) to bottom of Z3 for 1 min.] Repeat a total of 3 times	4 3	_____ _____	6
20–26	[Increase HR from the bottom of Z3 to midpoint of Z4 for 1 min., rpm 110 (11), (R) as needed. (Rec) to midpoint of Z3 for 1 min.] Repeat a total of 3 times	4 3	_____ _____	6
26–32	[Increase HR from midpoint of Z3 to bottom of Z5 for 1 min., rpm 110 (11), (R) as needed. (Rec) to bottom of Z4 for 1 min.] Repeat a total of 3 times	4 5	_____ _____	6
32–34	(Rec) to midpoint of Z3 for 1 min., then (rec) to midpoint of Z2 for 1 min.	3 2	_____ _____	2
34–38	[Increase HR from midpoint of Z2 to midpoint of Z3 in 1 min., rpm 60 (6), (R) as needed. (Rec) to midpoint of Z2 for 1 min.] Repeat	3 2	_____ _____	4
38–44	[Increase HR from the midpoint of Z2 to bottom of Z4 in 1 min., rpm 60 (6), (R) as needed. (Rec) to bottom of Z3 for 1 min.] Repeat a total of 3 times	4 3	_____ _____	6
44–50	[Increase HR from bottom of Z3 to midpoint of Z4 in 1 min., rpm 60 (6), (R) as needed. (Rec) to midpoint of Z3 for 1 min.] Repeat a total of 3 times	4 3	_____ _____	6
50–56	[Increase HR from midpoint of Z3 to bottom of Z5 in 1 min., rpm 60 (6), (R) as needed. (Rec) to bottom of Z4 for 1 min.] Repeat a total of 3 times	5 4	_____ _____	6
56–65	(Rec) to bottom of Z2, easy pedal and stretch	2	_____	9

WORKOUT 30. HALF RACK

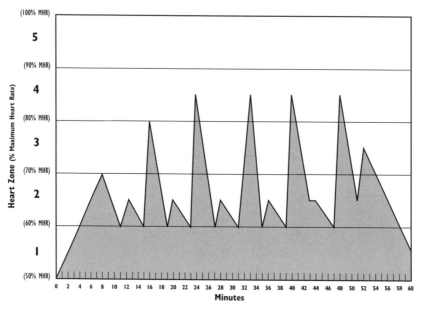

OVERVIEW

The best way to train on your bike for improved performance is to use your heart rate monitor as a coach. During this interval workout, use your monitor to give you biofeedback data; after all, that's one of its best uses. Whether you are training on or off the bike, focus on your monitor and use it as a window into your heart. When your mind and your muscles train together, in synchronicity, you'll find ultimate power. Let your mind interpret the heart rate number as you reach toward your peak heart rate and then recover back down.

DESCRIPTION

Half Rack is part training-ride and part cross-training workout as you alternate between riding on the bike and doing exercises off the bike. It makes the workout fun and full of variety. It is a total body workout and excellent for improving your overall fitness for other sports activities such as skiing, tennis, and swimming. Pick the heart zone you want to train in for the on-the-bike riding time; the off-the-bike exercises will range from Zone 2 to Zone 3.

STATS AND TIPS FOR WORKOUT 30: HALF RACK

Zone Number and Name	Minutes in Zone	Heart Zone Training Points	Estimated Calories
5. Red Line			
4. Threshold	15	60	180–210
3. Aerobic	3	9	27–33
2. Temperate	42	84	252–336
1. Healthy Heart			
Totals	**60**	**153**	**459–579**

SEQUENCE FOR WORKOUT 30: HALF RACK

Elapsed Time (min.)	Workout Plan	Heart Zone	Your Heart Rate (bpm)	Riding Time (min.)
0–8	Warm up to bottom of Z2, easy pedal	2	_____	8
8–12	[Isolated-leg training[a] (ILT): Right leg, moderate (R), 30 sec., then left leg, moderate (R), 30 sec.] Repeat a total of 3 times, finishing with a 1 min. (rec) as you get off the bike	3	_____	4
12–16	Situps for 3 min. Rest as needed. Vary position every min. You have 1 min. to get back on the bike and begin easy pedal	2	_____	4
16–20	[Surges: Moderate to heavy (R) for 45 sec., increase cadence for 15 sec.] Repeat a total of 3 times followed by 1 min. (rec) as you get off the bike	4	_____	4
20–24	Push-ups for 3 min. Rest as needed. 1 min. (rec) as you get back on the bike	2	_____	4
24–28	Lifts:[b] Moderate (R), 2 counts up, 2 counts down for 3 min. followed by 1 min. (rec) as you get off the bike	4	_____	4
28–32	Wall sit,[c] holding position for 3 min., rest as needed. Keep weight back over the heels. 1 min (rec) as you get back on the bike	2	_____	4
32–36	[Sprint, all-out effort for 30 sec., then 30 sec. (rec).] Repeat a total of 3 times followed by 1 min. (rec) as you get off the bike	4	_____	4
36–40	[Leg lifts:[d] Right leg 30 sec., left leg 30 sec.] Repeat a total of 3 times followed by 1 min. (rec) as you get back on the bike	2	_____	4
40–44	Standing climb, heavy (R), slow cadence, for 3 min. followed by 1 min. (rec) as you get off the bike	4	_____	4
44–48	[Triceps extension,[e] using hand weights from a kneeling position. Check form. Right arm 15 sec., rest 15 sec., left arm 15 sec., rest 15 sec.] Repeat a total of 3 times followed by 1 min. (rec) as you get back on the bike	2	_____	4
48–52	Power starts:[f] 15 sec. on, 15 sec. off, heavy (R), choice of standing or seated for 3 min., followed by 1 min. easy pedal (rec)	4	_____	4
52–60	Warm down and stretch	2	_____	8

[a] Pedaling with one leg at a time, resting the other on a box or stool. You may also choose to keep both feet in the pedals and allow one leg to relax while the other leg does the work.
[b] Alternating standing and seated positions done to a set count.
[c] Sitting with your back as flat as possible against a wall and upper legs 90 degrees to the floor. Hold this squat position for a period of time. Modify position if needed.
[d] Lying on your side, with a slight bend in the bottom leg, lift top leg up and then down, keeping the leg straight and working the inside and outside of the leg.
[e] From a bent-over position, grab the dumbbell with an overhand grip so that your palm is facing your body. The movement comes from the elbow joint (the shoulder does not rotate). Extend the working arm (squeeze the triceps—that is, the back of your upper arm) back straight behind you, but do not hyperextend. While controlling the weight, bend the elbow and return to the starting position. (From Ellen Karpay, *The Everything Total Fitness Book* [Adams Media Corporation, 2000, p. 154].)
[f] In a standing or seated position and from a slow spin, expend an all-out effort for 15 seconds by using heavy resistance or hard gearing followed by 15 seconds of recovery or easy pedaling. Alternate lead foot.

WORKOUT 31. HAPPY FEET

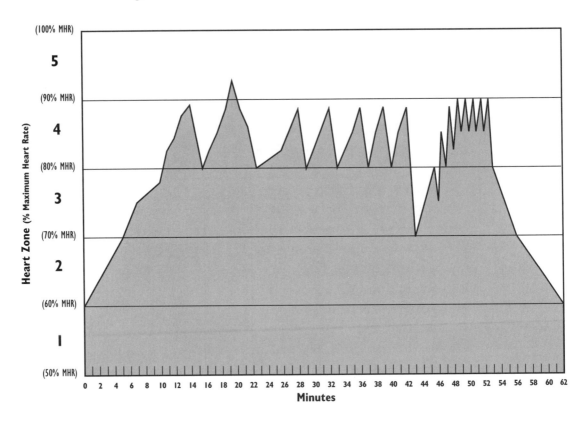

OVERVIEW

This is like getting a new pair of shoes—it makes your feet carefree! That's because when your feet are spinning and your heart is pumping, your heart rate monitor is displaying big happy numbers on its face. Happy Feet is full of variety and opportunities to use your imagination. Mentally take yourself outdoors to ride steep hills and fast descents. Focusing on small incremental differences in heart rate will make the time fly by and your feet even happier.

DESCRIPTION

Your goal is to raise your heart rate by using a smooth, fast spin as you concentrate on a quiet upper body and streamlined position. The heavy-resistance hill climbs should be done at 60 rpm or faster in the biggest gear that you can ride and hold your cadence in. The hill training develops muscular strength in either a standing or seated position. Ride the sprint intervals one of two ways: The first is a high-cadence, low-resistance approach, working on leg speed. The second is a slower-cadence, heavy-resistance (bigger gear) approach. Either way, keep those feet happy and pedaling.

STATS AND TIPS FOR WORKOUT 31: HAPPY FEET

Zone Number and Name	Minutes in Zone	Heart Zone Training Points	Estimated Calories
5. Red Line	6	30	90–120
4. Threshold	30	120	360–420
3. Aerobic	17	51	153–187
2. Temperate	9	18	54–72
1. Healthy Heart			
Totals	**62**	**219**	**657–799**

Tip: Use your heart rate monitor to diagnose your training rides. For example, if your heart rate stays high during recovery periods, it means something, but what it means depends on a number of factors that you will have to analyze. It might be a symptom that you are over-trained, did not warm up adequately, are not hydrated sufficiently, or your immune system might be impaired. (Refer to the *Heart Rate Monitor Book for Outdoor and Indoor Cyclists* [VeloPress, 2000] for more information on overtraining.)

SEQUENCE FOR WORKOUT 31: HAPPY FEET

Elapsed Time (min.)	Workout Plan	Heart Zone	Your Heart Rate (bpm)	Riding Time (min.)
0–7	Warm up gradually to bottom of Z3	3	_____	7
7–10	Increase HR to midpoint of Z3	3	_____	3
10–15	From midpoint of Z3 increase HR 5 bpm every min. for 5 min. by increasing cadence/rpm. Add (R) as needed	3 3 4 4 4	_____ _____ _____ _____ _____	5
15–16	Decrease HR to the bottom of Z4 for 1 min.	4	_____	1
16–26	From the bottom of Z4 add 5 bpm every min. using (R) and steady tempo. Once you reach Z5 decrease HR 5 bpm every min. to bottom of Z4	4 4	_____ _____	10
26–38	**Three-hill series:** [From bottom of Z4 increase HR 5 bpm with cadence for 2 min., then increase HR 10 bpm more with heavy (R) for 1 min. Decrease HR to bottom of Z4 for 1 min.] Repeat a total of 3 times	4 4 4	_____ _____ _____	12
38–44	**Two-hill series:** [From bottom of Z4 increase HR 10 bpm with heavy (R) for 1 min., then increase HR 5 bpm more with fast cadence for 1 min. Decrease HR to the bottom of Z4 for 1 min.] Repeat	4 4 4	_____ _____ _____	6
44–45	(Rec) to bottom of Z3 for 1 min.	3	_____	1
45–53	(8) 30 sec. sprints with 30 sec. (rec) starting from bottom of Z3 gradually increasing HR to bottom of Z5	3 5	_____ _____	8
53–62	Warm down to bottom of Z2, easy pedal and stretch	2	_____	9

WORKOUT 32. HOW 'BOUT THEM APPLES?

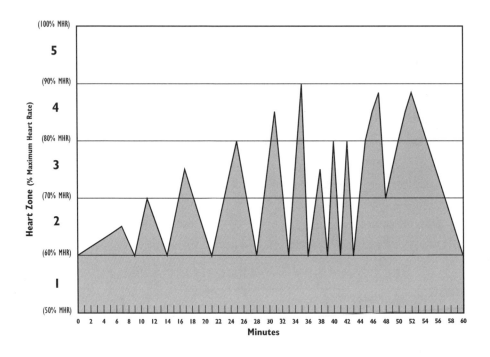

OVERVIEW

American colloquialisms usually originate from some event, and over time these sayings may lose their source. The origin of these Heart Zones Cycling workout names—like American colloquialisms—comes from some event that is connected to some activity. In this case, How 'Bout Them Apples originates from a comment made by Lance Armstrong during the Tour de France. Picture Lance powering past the peloton, taking the lead in one of the stages of the Tour in his yellow leaders' jersey. As he swept past the other riders, rumor has it, he turned to the closest rider and said, "How 'bout them apples?" As you take the lead, look around you and say to your fellow rider "How 'bout them apples" as your get fitter and faster.

DESCRIPTION

This workout combines isolated-leg training with two timed recoveries and two final ascents. The last two climbs build leg strength and power, two cycling components that we all need for improvement.

In the middle of the ride is a 2-minute complete-stop recovery heart rate test. Note your heart rate, then slowly decrease your cadence until you safely come to a complete stop and rest in the saddle for 2 minutes. Note the drop in your heart rate (the difference in the number of heartbeats per minute when you stopped pedaling and after resting for 2 minutes).

Later in the workout, you also do a 2-minute "active" or easy-pedal recovery, after which you should count the number of beats dropped. Retest in a month and compare your recovery heart rates. The faster your heart rate drops, the fitter you are.

STATS AND TIPS FOR WORKOUT 32: HOW 'BOUT THEM APPLES?

Zone Number and Name	Minutes in Zone	Heart Zone Training Points	Estimated Calories
5. Red Line	1	5	15–20
4. Threshold	11	44	132–154
3. Aerobic	12	36	108–132
2. Temperate	36	72	216–288
1. Healthy Heart			
Totals	60	157	471–594

Tip: To measure how much your fitness has improved, compare your recovery heart rate over time.

SEQUENCE FOR WORKOUT 32: HOW 'BOUT THEM APPLES?

Elapsed Time (min.)	Workout Plan	Heart Zone	Your Heart Rate (bpm)	Riding Time (min.)
0–7	Warm up to bottom of Z2 (60%), easy pedal	2	_____	7
7–9	Increase HR to midpoint of Z2, (65%)	2	_____	2
9–11	(Rec) to bottom of Z2 (60%)	2	_____	2
11–14	Isolated-leg training[a] (ILT): Increase HR to bottom of Z3 (70%) 1 min. for each leg followed by 1 min. easy pedal with both legs	3	_____	3
14–17	(Rec) to bottom of Z2, (60%), drink water	2	_____	3
17–21	Increase HR to midpoint of Z3 (75%), choice	3	_____	4
21–25	(Rec) to bottom of Z2 (60%), take a 2 min. test for recovery heart rate (RHR) by coming to a complete stop. Note the number of recovery heart beats in 2 min. Easy pedal for 2 min.	2	_____	4
25–28	Increase HR to bottom of Z4, (80%)	4	_____	3
28–31	(Rec) to bottom of Z2 (60%), stretch	2	_____	3
31–33	Increase HR to midpoint of Z4 (85%) in 2 min., choice	4	_____	2
33–35	(Rec) to bottom of Z2 (60%), 2 min. test for RHR, easy pedal rather than stop	2	_____	2
35–36	Increase HR to bottom of Z5 (90%) in 1 min., choice	5	_____	1
36–38	(Rec) to bottom of Z2 (60%)	2	_____	2
38–43	[Spin out,[b] add (R), spin out, (rec) to (60%).] Repeat for 5 min	2–4		5
43–45	(Rec) to bottom of Z2 (60%)	2	_____	2
45–55	[Standing run,[c] no (R), to bottom of Z4 in 1 min.; stay seated, increase HR to midpoint Z4 in 1 min.; standing, increase HR 5 bpm more for 1 min.; (rec) to bottom of Z2 for 2 min.] Repeat	4 4 4 2	_____ _____ _____	10
55–60	Warm down to bottom of Z2	2	_____	5

[a] Pedaling with one leg at a time, resting the other on a box or stool. You may also choose to keep both feet in the pedals and allow one leg to relax while the other leg does the work.

[b] Pedaling or spinning as fast as you can in one gear or at a certain resistance. Recover, then shift to a harder gear or resistance and again pedal as fast as you can. When you start to bounce on the seat and can no longer maintain a smooth and efficient pedal stroke, you have "spun out."

[c] Fast cadence in a standing position as if you are running up a hill.

WORKOUT 33. PUMPED

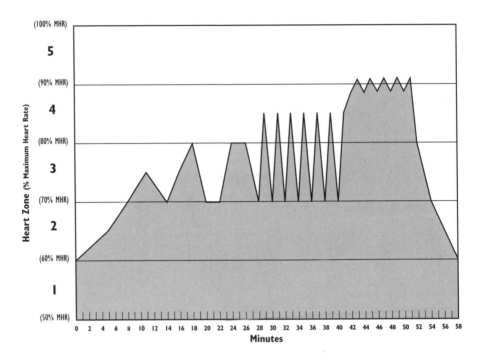

OVERVIEW

Circuit training is a highly effective way of exercising. Circuit skill training—such as the Pumped workout—on a bike is a specific application of the circuit training system. During each of five tough interval sets, you will work on a simulated circuit station, each featuring one of five different bike skills, with a recovery between each station. Each interval set involves working on a specific cycling skill and training effect. The benefit of training this way is that you improve your cycling skills, add variety to your workout, and get a great heart-pumping workout.

DESCRIPTION

There are five different stations in the Pumped circuit training workout:
- Interval 1: Strength circuit station
- Interval 2: Tempo circuit (steady-state) station
- Interval 3: Power circuit station
- Interval 4: Cadence circuit station
- Interval 5: Anaerobic threshold circuit station

During each interval, focus on the training method that applies to that interval. For example, when you are on the fourth interval, stay in the mindset throughout the 3-minute stress period of pedaling at a very high cadence. During the recovery period that follows each interval, stay in the relaxation and active-rest mindset to lower your heart rate as quickly as possible. One way to stay in the moment is to focus on the numbers on your monitor, which should be mounted on your handlebars. Your heart rate monitor should be pumped as well as your energy level when you finish this one!

Stats and Tips for Workout 33: Pumped

Zone Number and Name	Minutes in Zone	Heart Zone Training Points	Estimated Calories
5. Red Line	5	25	75–100
4. Threshold	20	80	240–280
3. Aerobic	23	69	207–253
2. Temperate	10	20	60–80
1. Healthy Heart			
Totals	58	194	582–713

Tip: Maximum sustainable heart rate is one of the best predictors of racing success.

Sequence for Workout 33: Pumped

Elapsed Time (min.)	Workout Plan	Heart Zone	Your Heart Rate (bpm)	Riding Time (min.)
0–5	Warm-up to bottom of Z2, easy pedal	2	_____	5
5–8	From bottom of Z2, increase HR 10 bpm, 90 rpm (9)	2	_____	3
8–14	Increase HR to bottom of Z3 and sustain for 3 min., then increase HR 10 more bpm for 3 min.	3	_____	6
14–24	Isolated-leg training[a] (ILT), changing legs every min., at 60 rpm (6) beginning at bottom of Z3 and increasing HR gradually by adding (R) to bottom of Z4	3 4	_____ _____	10
24–26	Pedal with both legs 60 rpm (6) to midpoint of Z4	4	_____	2
26–28	Super spin[b] at 120+ rpm (12), sustain at bottom of Z4	4	_____	2
28–29	Easy pedal (rec) to bottom of Z3	3	_____	1
29–37	[From a slow easy pedal, 1 min. fast, hard effort to mid-point of Z4 with heavy (R), followed by 1 min. easy pedal (rec) to bottom of Z3.] Repeat a total of 4 times	4 3	_____ _____	8
37–42	[From bottom of Z3, heavy (R) standing, 60 rpm (6), increase HR to midpoint of Z4 and sustain for 1 min., then easy pedal (rec), seated, to bottom of Z3, 90 rpm (9).] Repeat a total of 3 times	3 4	_____ _____	5
42–43	Increase HR to AT and sustain for 1 min.	4	_____	1
43–53	[Increase HR to 5 bpm above AT and sustain for 1 min., then decrease HR 5 bpm for 1 min.] Repeat 5 bpm interval a total of 5 times	4–5	_____	10
53–54	Decrease HR to bottom of Z4	4	_____	1
54–58	Decrease HR to bottom of Z3 for 2 min., then warm down to bottom of Z2	3 2	_____ _____	4

[a] Pedaling with one leg at a time, resting the other on a box or stool. You may also choose to keep both feet in the pedals and allow one leg to relax while the other leg does the work.

[b] High rpm or pedaling cadence. Usually 120 rpm or higher, keeping the pedal stroke smooth and efficient. Pedal only as fast as you can stay in control.

WORKOUT 34. SEATTLE RIDGE

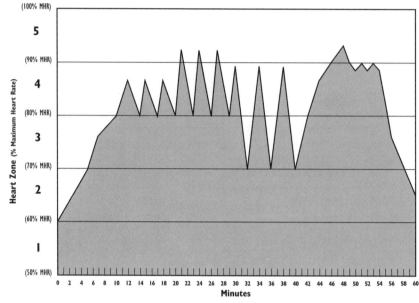

OVERVIEW

There are seven hills that adorn sea-level Seattle, Washington, one of the homes of Heart Zones Cycling. None of them, however, is named after Chief Seattle, the Native American who first encountered the white settlers of the Northwest. Rather, Seattle Ridge, a popular ski run, is located high in the mountains of Sun Valley, Idaho. Therefore, this is an appropriate name for a ride that feels like you are peddling at high altitude with a low concentration of the food that lungs crave—oxygen. If you feel the acidic taste of too much Red Line time, then you will have ridden this workout with total commitment. Baldy, the biggest ski mountain, is over 9000 feet high, and this ride gives you the sensation of climbing it from bottom to top more than once.

STATS FOR WORKOUT 34: SEATTLE RIDGE

Zone Number and Name	Minutes in Zone	Heart Zone Training Points	Estimated Calories
5. Red Line	12	60	180–240
4. Threshold	28	112	336–392
3. Aerobic	12	36	108–132
2. Temperate	8	16	48–64
1. Healthy Heart			
Totals	**60**	**224**	**672–828**

Tip: Overreaching is a way of exercising at high training loads but without reaching a point of damage as in overtraining. For even more information on overtraining, an excellent resource is Jon Ackland's book *Power to Perform: A Comprehensive Guide to Training and Racing for Endurance Athletes* (Reed Publishing, New Zealand, 1996; pp. 133–140).

DESCRIPTION

Most riders love the Seattle Ridge workout because one-third of the riding time is in the Threshold and the Red Line Zones—Zones 4 and 5. Every rider pays a price for hanging out in such high and hot zones. That price is totally individual—so watch for the symptoms of too much high-intensity training. As you ride Seattle Ridge's 20- and 40-bpm intervals, choose between using speed or resistance to ascend and descend each one. For an even harder ride, raise your front wheel 4 to 6 inches off the ground by putting a support underneath the wheel or the bike frame. The result resembles the more acute feeling of climbing steep hills.

SEQUENCE FOR WORKOUT 34: SEATTLE RIDGE

Elapsed Time (min.)	Workout Plan	Heart Zone	Your Heart Rate (bpm)	Riding Time (min.)
0–5	Warm up to bottom of Z2 (60%), easy pedal	2	_____	5
5–10	Increase HR gradually to midpoint of Z3 (75%) with cadence/rpm	3	_____	5
10–14	**10 bpm interval:** Increase HR to the bottom of Z4 for 2 min., steady cadence, increase (R). Increase HR to midpoint of Z4 (85%) for 2 min., steady cadence, increase (R). Seated	4 4	_____ _____	4
14–20	[(Rec) to bottom of Z4 for 1 min., easy pedal, then increase HR to midpoint of Z4 for 2 min. using (R), steady cadence.] Repeat	4 4	_____ _____	6
20–29	**20 bpm interval:** [Increase HR from bottom of Z4 to bottom of Z5 in 2 min., using (R), steady cadence. (rec) to bottom of Z4 in 1 min., easy pedal.] Repeat a total of 3 times	5 4	_____ _____	9
29–43	**40 bpm interval:** [Increase HR to bottom of Z5 in 2 min., sprint with (R). (Rec) to bottom of Z3 in 2 min., easy pedal.] Repeat a total of 3 times	5 3	_____ _____	14
43–44	Increase HR to bottom of Z4, choice	4	_____	1
44–46	Increase HR 10 bpm to midpoint of Z4, choice	4	_____	2
46–48	Increase HR to bottom of Z5, choice	5	_____	2
48–49	All-out sprint for peak HR	5	_____	1
49–55	Decrease HR to bottom of Z5 for 1 min., then decrease HR 5 bpm more for 1 min., then increase 5 bpm for 1 min. Drop 5 bpm for 1 min., add 5 bpm for 1 min., and finally drop 5 bpm for 1 min.	5 4	_____ _____	6
55–60	Decrease 10 bpm every minute as warm down into Z2	2	_____	5

WORKOUT 35. SIX-PACK

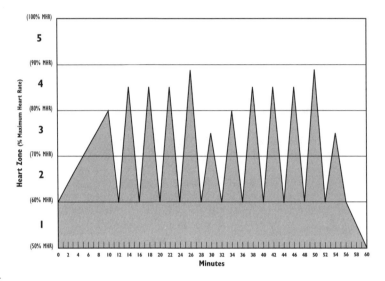

OVERVIEW

Nicknames are fun, especially if they stick because they fit. Workouts share that with nicknames. One of our business partners in the Heart Zones Cycling company has struggled with her friends affectionately calling her "Six-Pack" because it connotes one of two different meanings. The first is six containers of a beverage usually containing hops as the primary ingredient. The insinuation here is obvious. The other meaning for the word "six-pack" is applied to an individual whose abdominal muscles are so defined that they resemble the curved pattern of a washboard.

STATS AND TIPS FOR WORKOUT 35: SIX-PACK

Zone Number and Name	Minutes in Zone	Heart Zone Training Points	Estimated Calories
5. Red Line			
4. Threshold	20	80	240–280
3. Aerobic	9	27	81–99
2. Temperate	29	58	174–232
1. Healthy Heart	2	2	6–10
Totals	60	167	501–621

Tip: During your recovery intervals, count the number of beats per minute you can drop in 2 minutes. The higher the number, the better indication that you are fit. This is a standard recovery heart rate protocol.

DESCRIPTION

Six-Pack is a good workout for anyone suffering from the monotony syndrome. That's a situation of poor performance usually as a result of boredom or lack of variety in your workouts. Symptoms of monotony include missed workouts, disinterest in riding, and a low energy when riding the bike. Six-Pack is a series of six individual 4-minute intervals that are repeated. You set the heart rate number—

in this case the peak heart rate number—for the interval sets. Stay in the Aerobic Zone, 70–80% of your maximum heart rate, if you want to get fit. Take the higher Zone 4 or even Zone 5 if you are a competitive athlete. Recover in Zone 2, the Temperate Zone, after each work interval.

SEQUENCE FOR WORKOUT 35: SIX-PACK

Elapsed Time (min.)	Workout Plan	Heart Zone	Your Heart Rate (bpm)	Riding Time (min.)
0–5	Warm up to bottom of Z2, easy pedal	2	_____	5
5–10	Increase HR to bottom of Z3	3	_____	5
10–12	[Surges:[a] Moderate to heavy (R) for 45 sec. then increase cadence for 15 sec.] Repeat	4	_____	2
12–14	Easy pedal (rec) for 2 min. to Z2	2	_____	2
14–18	Power starts:[b] 15 sec. hard effort, 15 sec. easy for 2 min. followed by 2 min. easy pedal (rec) to Z2.	4 2	_____ _____	4
18–22	Standing climb:[c] Heavy (R), slow cadence, steady cadence for 2 min., followed by 2 min. easy pedal (rec) to Z2	4 2	_____ _____	4
22–26	Sprint:[d] Fast pedal, 120 rpm (12), followed by 2 min. easy pedal (rec) to Z2	4 2	_____ _____	4
26–30	Lifts:[e] Moderate (R), 2 counts (sec.) standing, 2 counts (sec.) seated for 2 min. followed by easy pedal 2 min. (rec) to Z2	4 2	_____ _____	4
30–32	[Isolated-leg training[f] (ILT): Right leg, moderate (R) for 30 sec. followed by left leg, moderate (R) for 30 sec.] Repeat	3	_____	2
32–34	2 min. easy pedal (rec) to Z2	2	_____	2
34–38	Repeat 2 min. of surges and 2 min. (rec)	4 2	_____ _____	4
38–42	Repeat 2 min. power starts and 2 min. (rec)	4 2	_____ _____	4
42–46	Repeat 2 min. standing climb and 2 min. (rec)	4 2	_____ _____	4
46–50	Repeat 2 min. sprint and 2 min. (rec)	4 2	_____ _____	4
50–54	Repeat 2 min. jumps and 2 min. (rec)	4 2	_____ _____	4
54–58	Repeat 2 min. ILT and 2 min. (rec)	3	_____	4
58–60	Warm down to bottom of Z2	2		2

[a]Moderate to heavy resistance with cadence changes.
[b]In a standing or seated position and from a slow spin, expend an all-out effort for 15 seconds by using heavy resistance or hard gearing followed by 15 seconds of recovery or easy pedaling. Alternate lead foot.
[c]Standing position on the bike with heavy resistance or hard gearing. Keep body weight over the legs and a light touch on the handlebars.
[d]All-out effort with enough resistance or gearing to stay in control and not bounce on the seat.
[e]Alternate riding in a standing position and a seated position. Usually done to a count or seconds.
[f]Pedal with only one leg, resting the other on a box or stool, or simply keep your feet in the pedals and allow one leg to relax while the other does the work.

WORKOUT 36. SPENTERVALS

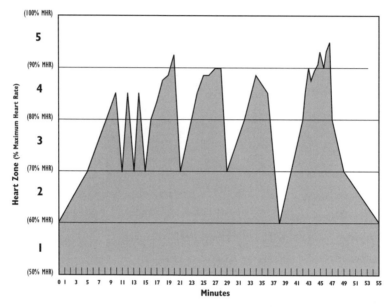

OVERVIEW

If you love to party hard and suffer the next day from the festivities, Spentervals might be your training ride. This workout is guaranteed to make you feel totally "spent" when you're done. It's one of those hang-your-tongue-out-and-gasp-for-air training rides that is meant only for those who are in top shape. It truly is a grand tour of five different workouts that melt into one that then melts you down: killer intervals, tempo gusto, speed sprints, Super Spins, and a 5-kilometer time trial to the finish banner 60 minutes later.

DESCRIPTION

This ride is pure Zone 4 with 50% of your riding time there and another 50% of your time in red-hot Zone 5. Because it's high and hot, the 48-hour rule automatically goes into effect. That means you need to take a 48-hour break from riding in the high heart zones afterward to allow for adequate between-day or interworkout recovery. The muscle and fuel recovery process takes approximately 48 hours, so take a break or do a short active recovery workout in the lower zones.

STATS AND TIPS FOR WORKOUT 36: SPENTERVALS

Zone Number and Name	Minutes in Zone	Heart Zone Training Points	Estimated Calories
5. Red Line	7	35	105–140
4. Threshold	20	80	240–280
3. Aerobic	16	48	144–176
2. Temperate	12	24	72–96
1. Healthy Heart			
Totals	**55**	**187**	**561–692**

SEQUENCE FOR WORKOUT 36: SPENTERVALS

Elapsed Time (min.)	Workout Plan	Heart Zone	Your Heart Rate (bpm)	Riding Time (min.)
0–5	Warm up to bottom of Z2, easy pedal	2	_____	5
5–10	Increase HR to bottom of Z3	3	_____	5
10–16	[From bottom of Z3 increase HR 30 bpm, hard effort, 100 rpm (10) for 1 min., then (rec) to bottom of Z3 in 1 min., easy pedal.] Repeat a total of 3 times	4 3 4 3 4 3	_____ _____ _____ _____ _____ _____	6
16–17	From bottom of Z3, 1 min. sprint to bottom of Z4	4	_____	1
17–21	From bottom of Z4 holding a steady cadence of 80 rpm (8), increase HR 5 bpm every min. for 4 min. Stay seated	4 4 4/5	_____ _____ _____	4
21–23	(Rec) to bottom of Z3. Drink water and stretch	3	_____	2
23–28	[10 sec. hard effort, standing, (R), then 10 sec. easy pedal, seated.] Repeat interval a total of 15 times or 5 min. total	4 4 5	_____ _____ _____	5
28–30	(Rec) to bottom of Z3. Drink more water	3	_____	2
30–42	[30 sec. all-out sprint, then 30 sec. easy pedal (rec).] Repeat interval a total of 12 times, alternating standing and seated	4 4 4	_____ _____ _____	12
42–45	(Rec) to bottom of Z2. Drink water! Mentally prepare for 5K time trial.	2	_____	3
45–50	5-min., 5K time trial: Use your imagination and create your own 5 min. race scenario, riding at AT with a final 1 min. sprint to the finish line.	4 4 5	_____ _____ _____	5
50–55	Warm down to bottom of Z2	2	_____	5

Note: A time-trial race is you against the clock. Stay motivated by mentally creating the race scenario or use the following imagery: The time trial begins with a fast, hard effort off the starting line for 1 minute to the beginning of the first 1-minute hill. The first 30 seconds of the hill is seated with a fast cadence (120 rpm). The last 30 seconds of the hill is in a standing position with heavy resistance or big gears, powering yourself up and over the top. In the slight downhill that follows, you decrease only 3 bpm every 30 seconds and sustain 80 rpm (adjust resistance or gearing as needed to maintain heart rate). Next is a Super Spin flat section of 120 rpm or faster for 30 seconds. Keep your heart rate at or above your anaerobic threshold with a final all-out 1-minute sprint to the finish line. Once you have crossed the finish line, look at your monitor and don't be surprised if it continues to go up for a few seconds and you reach "peak heart" rate for the workout.

WORKOUT 37. SUN VALLEY EXPRESS

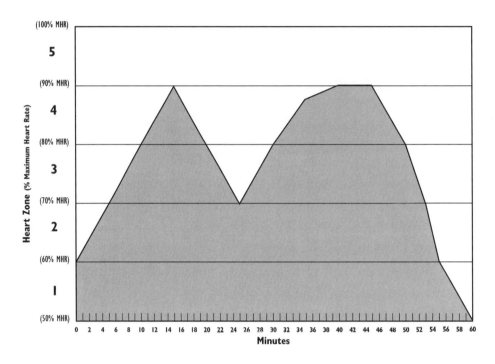

OVERVIEW

One day as she rode the lift to the top of one of the black-diamond alpine ski runs in Sun Valley, Idaho, Sally Reed dreamed of writing and then riding a black diamond workout. The Sun Valley Express is the product of her mind creating cycling workouts as she exploded down steep and deep bowls of light fluffy powder.

On your next workout, why don't you dedicate it to creating a workout, writing it, riding it, and then sharing it with us by contacting us at www.heartzones.com? May your experience of creation bring to you the joy that Sun Valley Express gives Sally each time she rides it on her bike or schusses downhill on her skis.

DESCRIPTION

The goal of this workout is to finish it. When you do, you have trained your physiology to adapt to an increased effort of pedaling at a high cadence and workload. The pyramid climb should be done at cadences over 100 rpm to train your legs to become more fatigue-resistant at high pedaling rates. As you increase your leg speed, keep your pedal stroke smooth without bouncing on the saddle or allowing your hips to rock. Pull through the bottom of the stroke and over the top, making the stroke as round as possible. At minute 20 on this ride, there's one 10-minute recovery period that gives you a much needed rest. Recover to the bottom of Heart Zone 3, the Aerobic Zone, down to 70% of your maximum heart rate. Few black diamond workouts on skis or a bike give you much recovery until you reach the bottom or finish the course.

STATS AND TIPS FOR WORKOUT 37: SUN VALLEY EXPRESS

Zone Number and Name	Minutes in Zone	Heart Zone Training Points	Estimated Calories
5. Red Line	19	95	285–380
4. Threshold	20	80	240–280
3. Aerobic	13	39	117–143
2. Temperate	8	16	48–64
1. Healthy Heart			
Totals	**60**	**230**	**690–867**

Tip: Your heart zones are unique to you and anchored by your maximum heart rate. Do not compare your absolute heart rate number with that of someone else; rather, compare your relative or percentage of maximum heart rate.

SEQUENCE FOR WORKOUT 37: SUN VALLEY EXPRESS

Elapsed Time (min.)	Workout Plan	Heart Zone	Your Heart Rate (bpm)	Riding Time (min.)
0–5	Warm up to bottom of Z2	2	_____	5
5–10	Increase HR to bottom of Z3	3	_____	5
10–15	Increase HR to bottom of Z4, choice	4	_____	5
15–20	Increase HR to bottom of Z5, choice	5	_____	5
20–25	Decrease HR to bottom of Z4, choice	4	_____	5
25–30	Decrease HR to bottom of Z3, choice	3	_____	5
30–50	Pyramid climb[a]: Begin with a 15 sec. fast pedal (100–130 rpm) (10–13), then 30 sec. easy pedal (rec). Repeat using the following times:	3	_____	20
	30 sec. fast pedal, then 30 sec. (rec) 45 sec. fast pedal, then 30 sec. (rec)	3	_____	
	60 sec. fast pedal, then 30 sec. (rec) 1:15 fast pedal, then 30 sec. (rec)	4	_____	
	1:30 fast pedal, then 30 sec. (rec) 1:45 fast pedal, then 30 sec. (rec)	4	_____	
	2:00 fast pedal, then 30 sec. (rec) 1:45 fast pedal, then 30 sec. (rec)	5	_____	
	1:30 fast pedal, then 30 sec. (rec) 1:15 fast pedal, then 30 sec. (rec)	5	_____	
	60 sec. fast pedal, then 30 sec. (rec) 45 sec. fast pedal, then 30 sec. (rec)	4	_____	
	30 sec. fast pedal, then 30 sec. (rec) 15 sec. fast pedal, then 30 sec. (rec)	4	_____	
50–60	Easy pedal warm down to Z2	2	_____	10

[a]Incremental increases and decreases in time and intensity. Think of climbing up and down a hill.

WORKOUT 38. THE RIGHT STUFF

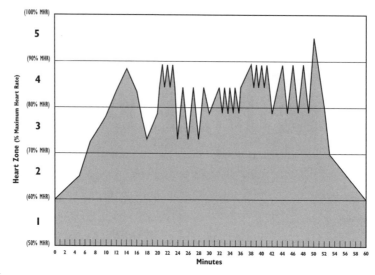

OVERVIEW

Ever wonder if you're made of the right stuff? Do you have what it takes? Do doubts pop into your head before a big race or a challenging workout? When your too-often companion, the imaginary monkey of self doubt, jumps on your back and you hear it whisper in your ear, "What are you doing here?" just say to yourself, "I have the right stuff." And, after you finish The Right Stuff, you can toss that monkey off your back, throw your shoulders back, and breathe deeply because you have proven it by finishing this ride.

DESCRIPTION

This workout is a series of 10- and 20-bpm intervals using fast sprints and steep hills. The workout tests your ability to respond quickly and with vigor to the workload and the recovery-time requirements. Practice sprinting skills along with heavy-resistance climbs. Vary your standing and seated positions to work specific muscle groups. As you ride, keep focused on the right stuff—your heart rate monitor and your heart.

STATS AND TIPS FOR WORKOUT 38: THE RIGHT STUFF

Zone Number and Name	Minutes in Zone	Heart Zone Training Points	Estimated Calories
5. Red Line	2	10	30–40
4. Threshold	27	108	324–378
3. Aerobic	19	57	171–209
2. Temperate	12	24	72–96
1. Healthy Heart			
Totals	60	199	597–723

Tip: Try sprinting out of the saddle to your highest revolutions per minute; then sit down and sustain that same number of revolutions per minute.

SEQUENCE FOR WORKOUT 38: THE RIGHT STUFF

Elapsed Time (min.)	Workout Plan	Heart Zone	Your Heart Rate (bpm)	Riding Time (min.)
0–5	Warm up to bottom of Z2, easy pedal	2	_____	5
5–7	Increase HR to midpoint of Z2, cadence/rpm for 2 min.	2	_____	2
7–10	Increase HR to bottom of Z3, cadence/rpm for 3 min.	3	_____	3
10–16	Increase HR to midpoint of Z3 in 2 min., choice;	3	_____	6
	increase HR to bottom of Z4 in 2 min., choice;	4	_____	
	increase HR to midpoint of Z4 in 2 min., (R)	4	_____	
16–18	Decrease HR 10 bpm every min. for 2 min.	4	_____	2
		3	_____	
18–20	Decrease HR to max. HR minus 50 bpm for 2 min.	3	_____	2
20–21.5	Increase HR 10 bpm every 30 sec. (3 times), choice	3	_____	1.5
		4	_____	
		4	_____	
21.5–23	Decrease HR 10 bpm for 30 sec., then increase	4	_____	1.5
	HR 10 bpm for 30 sec., and decrease	4	_____	
	HR 10 bpm for 30 sec.	4	_____	
23–29	[Decrease HR to max. HR minus 50 bpm for	3	_____	6
	1 min., then increase HR 20 bpm for 1 min.]	4	_____	
	Repeat a total of 3 times			
29–32	Decrease HR to max. HR minus 40 bpm for 3 min.	3	_____	3
32–36	[Increase HR 10 bpm for 30 sec., then decrease HR	4	_____	4
	10 bpm for 30 sec.] Repeat a total of 4 times	3	_____	
36–38	Increase HR to max. HR minus 30 bpm for 2 min.	4	_____	2
38–42	[Increase HR 10 bpm for 30 sec., then decrease HR	4	_____	4
	10 bpm for 30 sec.] Repeat a total of 4 times	4	_____	
42–44	Decrease HR to max. HR minus 40 bpm for 2 min.	3	_____	2
44–50	[Increase HR 20 bpm for 1 min., then decrease HR	4	_____	6
	20 bpm for 1 min.] Repeat a total of 3 times	4	_____	
50–52	All-out sprint to peak heart rate for 2 min.	5	_____	2
52–53	Decrease HR to bottom of Z4	4	_____	1
53–55	Decrease HR to bottom of Z3	3	_____	2
55–60	Warm down to bottom of Z2, easy pedal	2	_____	5

WORKOUT 39. TIME-TRIAL TERROR

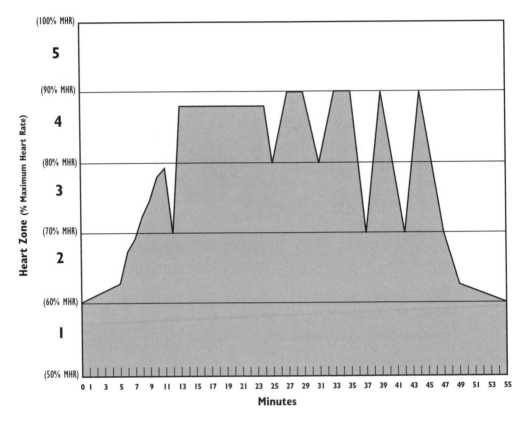

OVERVIEW

A time trial is an event or workout that allows you to compete with yourself against the clock. The drive to do better when time trialing is internal rather than the external motivation of racing against other cyclists. There are a number of skills required to be a proficient time-trial cyclist including pacing yourself, specific training that fits the requirements of the event, aerodynamics, and internal motivation. This is a time-trial ride that trains you in the specific skills necessary to become a terror as a time-trial rider.

STATS AND TIPS FOR WORKOUT 39: TIME-TRIAL TERROR

Zone Number and Name	Minutes in Zone	Heart Zone Training Points	Estimated Calories
5. Red Line	14	70	210–280
4. Threshold	12	48	168–144
3. Aerobic	15	45	135–165
2. Temperate	14	28	84–112
1. Healthy Heart			
Totals	**55**	**191**	**597–701**

Tip: Take the stress off of your knees by riding easier gears or resistance at a higher cadence.

DESCRIPTION

You choose the gearing or resistance that is the best for workload efficiency. If you choose to ride bigger gears or heavier resistance at a lower cadence, then practice that during the intervals. Or choose the opposite—ride an easier gear or less resistance, at a higher cadence. Pedaling at a higher cadence with the same resistance requires a higher aerobic capacity and elicits a higher heart rate. The key here is the word *sustain*. If you fatigue before the interval is complete, you need to lower your heart rate numbers.

SEQUENCE FOR WORKOUT 39: TIME-TRIAL TERROR

Elapsed Time (min.)	Workout Plan	Heart Zone	Your Heart Rate (bpm)	Riding Time (min.)
0–6	Warm up to bottom of Z2, easy pedal	2	_____	6
6–12	Increase cadence to 90 rpm (9) for 1 min., then each min. increase cadence by 10 rpm up to 140 rpm (14) for a total of 6 min.	3	_____	6
12–13	(Rec) to bottom of Z3	3	_____	1
13–25	A series of (12) 1 min. intervals. Your choice of option 1 or option 2: **Option 1:** (12) 1 min. intervals, moderate to heavy (R), 70 rpm (7) for 45 sec. followed by 15 sec. at 90 rpm (9). HR at midpoint of Z4 or higher **Option 2:** (12) 1 min. intervals, moderate (R), 100 rpm (10) for 45 sec. followed by 15 sec. at 120 rpm (12)	4	_____	12
25–27	(Rec) to bottom of Z3	3	_____	2
27–39	[4 min. interval, heavy (R), seated, 85 rpm (8–9) to bottom of Z5, then 2 min. (rec) to bottom of Z3.] Repeat	5 3 5 3	_____ _____ _____ _____	12
39–49	[3 min. interval, heavy (R), standing, 90 rpm (9) to bottom of Z5, then 2 min. (rec) to bottom of Z3.] Repeat	5 3 5 3	_____ _____ _____ _____	10
49–55	Warm down to Z2, easy pedal	2	_____	6

WORKOUT 40. TOP GUN

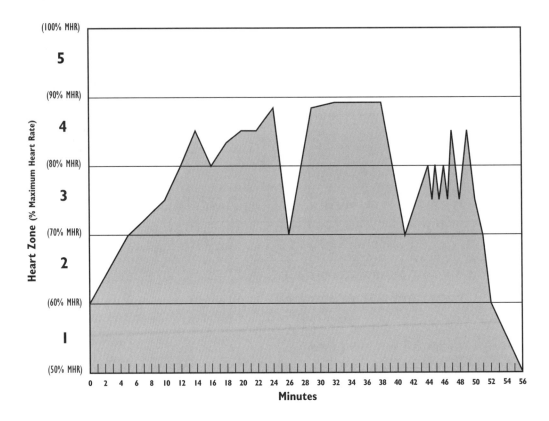

OVERVIEW

Flying a new jet fighter and riding a sleek studio bike share some common features. In the movie *Top Gun*, Tom Cruise maneuvers through dogfights and love experiences. On this ride, you are the "Top Gun," flying into the stratosphere, pedaling fast and hard, speeding on your bike from start to finish. In this ride, you leave more than your mark; you also leave a pool of sweat.

DESCRIPTION

There are five riding experiences buried in the heart of this workout. The first experience is to slow spin with low revolutions per minute to build endurance. Second, you transition into heavy resistance or big gears to develop riding power by using a series of quick accelerations from a standing position. The third experience challenges your anaerobic threshold heart rate as you select the highest heart rate you can sustain for a 12-minute period. Stare at your monitor and lock onto that number. The next to last, or fourth, experience is rapid spinning to develop speed. The finale is to push the throttle stick with heavy resistance and a cadence change for power pacing. When you finish the workout Top Gun, you are the star of your own show, your own ride.

STATS AND TIPS FOR WORKOUT 40: TOP GUN

Zone Number and Name	Minutes in Zone	Heart Zone Training Points	Estimated Calories
5. Red Line			
4. Threshold	29	116	348–406
3. Aerobic	18	54	162–198
2. Temperate	7	14	42–56
1. Healthy Heart	2	2	6–10
Totals	**56**	**186**	**558–670**

Tip: In large part, it's the feeling of finishing a workout strong, like a Top Gun, that propels us to ride again.

SEQUENCE FOR WORKOUT 40: TOP GUN

Elapsed Time (min.)	Workout Plan	Heart Zone	Your Heart Rate (bpm)	Riding Time (min.)
0–5	Warm up to bottom of Z2, easy pedal	2	_____	5
5–10	Increase HR to bottom of Z3	3	_____	5
10–16	From the bottom of Z3, hold 60 rpm (6), increase resistance (R) every 2 min. to bottom of Z4	3 4 4	_____ _____ _____	6
16–18	Sustain bottom of Z4 with a fast spin, 100 rpm (10)	4	_____	2
18–26	[Power starts:[a] From a standing position and slow spin, heavy (R), 10 sec. quick acceleration followed by 20 sec. seated (rec).] Repeat a total of 16 times or 8 min.	4	_____	8
26–29	Decrease HR to bottom of Z3, easy pedal. Drink water	3	_____	3
29–41	Anaerobic threshold training:[b] Pick an HR number that you can sustain for 12 min. Change body and hand positions frequently	4 or higher	_____	12
41–44	Decrease HR to bottom of Z3, easy pedal. Drink water	3	_____	3
44–47	[Spin ups:[c] From 60 rpm (6) to 120 rpm (12) in 30 sec., then 30 sec. (rec). Smooth pedaling, add resistance or change gearing as needed.] Repeat a total of 3 times	4 3	_____ _____	3
47–51	[Surges:[d] Steady tempo for 45 sec. with heavy (R), increase cadence for 15 sec., followed by 1 min. (rec).] Repeat	4	_____	4
51–56	Warm down to Z2 then Z1	2 1	_____ _____	5

[a] From a slow spin or stopped position, seated or standing, and with heavy resistance, expend an all-out effort for 10 seconds followed by a 20-second recovery or easy pedaling. Alternate lead legs.

[b] Maintaining your highest sustainable heart rate for a period of time. Typically, the higher the percentage of your maximum heart rate you can sustain, the fitter you are.

[c] Increase cadence progressively by 5 to 10 rpm at regular intervals, keeping the pedal stroke smooth and efficient.

[d] Moderate to heavy resistance with cadence increases.

WORKOUT 41. UNLEASH THE MOJO!

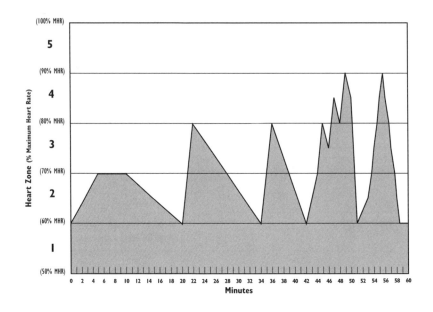

OVERVIEW

Like a great cup of coffee, this Red Line workout gives you more than a caffeine boost—it is one big dose of high intensity with a high number of heart zone training points. In 1 hour, you accumulate almost 200 points. This means that in one day you have exercised enough to almost qualify for a week's worth of exercise as recommended by the American College of Sports Medicine (ACSM).

DESCRIPTION

During the first half of the Mojo workout, the ride focuses on improving your leg speed with a smooth pedal stroke. Work each leg in the isolated-leg interval to exhaustion before switching to the other leg. During the ride, you get a total of 10 minutes of isolated-leg training. The second half of the Mojo ride focuses on developing your leg strength and sprint capability. The final pick-up toward the end of the ride is a pyramid, ascending 10 bpm every 30 seconds until you hit 90% of maximum heart rate, and then descending back down the same way.

STATS AND TIPS FOR WORKOUT 41: UNLEASH THE MOJO!

Zone Number and Name	Minutes in Zone	Heart Zone Training Points	Estimated Calories
5. Red Line	2	10	30–40
4. Threshold	24	96	288–336
3. Aerobic	19	57	171–209
2. Temperate	15	30	90–120
1. Healthy Heart			
Totals	**60**	**193**	**579–705**

Tip: Isolating the pedaling action can result in a smoother, more efficient spin.

SEQUENCE FOR WORKOUT 41: UNLEASH THE MOJO!

Elapsed Time (min.)	Workout Plan	Heart Zone	Your Heart Rate (bpm)	Riding Time (min.)
0–5	Warm up to bottom of Z2 (60%)	2	_____	5
5–10	Spin ups:[a] Gradually increase rpm to maximum cadence for 1 min., light (R), followed by 15 sec. (rec). Repeat a total of 4 times	3	_____	5
10–20	Isolated-leg training [b] (ILT): Start with either leg, fast cadence with light to moderate (R). Change to other leg when fatigued.	3	_____	10
20–22	(Rec) to bottom of Z2 (60%)	2	_____	2
22–34	10 sec. seated sprint, little or no (R), followed by a 50 sec. easy pedal (rec). Repeat interval in standing position. And so on . . . 15 sec. seated sprint, 45 sec. (rec). Repeat standing 20 sec. seated sprint, 40 sec. (rec). Repeat standing 25 sec. seated sprint, 35 sec. (rec). Repeat standing 30 sec. seated sprint, 30 sec. (rec). Repeat standing 35 sec. seated sprint, 25 sec. (rec). Repeat standing	4	_____	12
34–36	(Rec) bottom of Z2	2	_____	2
36–42	From the bottom of Z2, 60 rpm (6), moderate to heavy (R), 45 sec., increase rpm last 15 sec. leaving (R) the same. Repeat a total of 6 times	2 4	_____ _____	6
42–44	(Rec) to bottom of Z2	2	_____	2
44–45	Increase HR to bottom of Z3 (70%) in 1 min., choice	3	_____	1
45–47	From bottom of Z3 increase HR to bottom of Z4 in 1 min., then (rec) to midpoint of Z3 for 1 min.	3 4/3	_____ _____	2
47–49	From midpoint of Z3 increase HR to midpoint of Z4 in 1 min., then (rec) to bottom of Z4 for 1 min.	3 4	_____ _____	2
49–51	From bottom of Z4 increase HR to bottom of Z5 in 1 min., then (rec) to midpoint of Z4 for 1 min.	5 4	_____ _____	2
51–53	(Rec) to bottom of Z2	2	_____	2
53–60	From the bottom of Z2 (60%) increase HR 10 bpm or in 5% increments every 30 sec. to bottom of Z5 (i.e., 60%, 65%, 70%, 75%, 80%, 85%, 90%) then back down 10 bpm or in 5% increments to bottom of Z2 (60%), choice	2 3 4 5 4 3 2	_____ _____ _____ _____ _____ _____ _____	7

[a] Increase the cadence progressively by 5 to 10 rpm at regular intervals. Keep the pedal stroke smooth and efficient.
[b] Pedal with only one leg; rest the other on a box or stool. You may also keep your feet on the pedals and allow one leg to relax while the other leg does the work.

WORKOUT 42. WHITE KNUCKLES

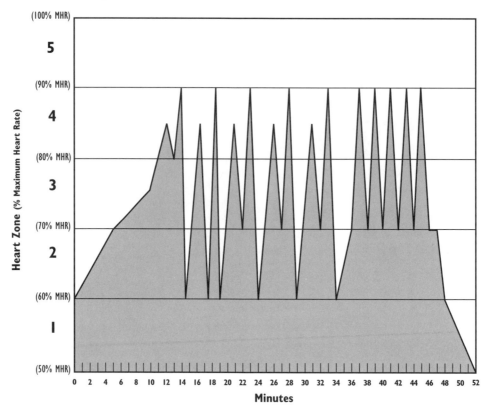

OVERVIEW

Imagine riding down a fast descent on a cold and wet day, spinning in pure-fatigue mode at the end of a long, hard, ride—and you start to lose control. Your hands have squeezed the blood out of themselves as you grip the handlebars, hanging on for dear life. White Knuckles is that kind of ride. Relax. It's just another day in paradise.

Sally Edwards (center) rides White Knuckles at the Bellevue Club in Bellevue, Washington, with club members (from left to right) Wally Prestbo, Marilyn Caplan, Mark Allison, and Suzanne Strom Reed.

DESCRIPTION

You face the climb of five hills within the first 30 minutes of this workout. Hills are great because they build your leg strength as you climb up and then transition to improving your leg speed as you spin down the backside. You may choose to stay seated or work on your standing climbs. Concentrate on a fast but smooth pedal stroke on the sprints and a relaxed upper body. Check your knuckles and if they are turning white as you ride up and down your heart zones, remember to relax. Finish the last 10 minutes with sprints to the bottom of Zone 5 and recoveries to the bottom of Zone 3. See how many sprints to 90% of maximum heart rate (the floor of Zone 5) and recoveries to 60% of your maximum heart rate (the floor of Zone 3) you can complete in 10 minutes.

STATS AND TIPS FOR WORKOUT 42: WHITE KNUCKLES

Zone Number and Name	Minutes in Zone	Heart Zone Training Points	Estimated Calories
5. Red Line	9	45	135–180
4. Threshold	5	20	60–70
3. Aerobic	19	57	171–209
2. Temperate	17	34	102–136
1. Healthy Heart	2	2	6–10
Totals	52	158	474–605

Tip: Perceived exertion rate and heart rate vary tremendously when your knuckles turn white.

SEQUENCE FOR WORKOUT 42: WHITE KNUCKLES

Elapsed Time (min.)	Workout Plan	Heart Zone	Your Heart Rate (bpm)	Riding Time (min.)
0–5	Warm up to bottom of Z2, easy pedal	2	_____	5
5–10	Increase HR to bottom of Z3, choice	3	_____	5
10–12	Increase HR to midpoint of Z3, choice	3	_____	2
12–37	[Increase HR to midpoint of Z4 for 1 min.,	4	_____	25
	heavy (R), 70 rpm (7), followed by a 1 min. (rec)	3	_____	
	to bottom of Z3 then a 1 min. sprint to bottom	5	_____	
	of Z5. Finish with a 2 min. (rec) to bottom of Z2.]	2	_____	
	Repeat a total of 5 times			
37–38	Increase HR to bottom of Z3	3	_____	1
38–48	Ups and downs[a] from bottom of Z3 to bottom of	3	_____	10
	Z5 and (rec) to bottom of Z3. Count the number	5	_____	
	of times you can do this interval in 10 min.	3	_____	
48–52	(Rec) to bottom of Z3, then bottom of Z2,	3	_____	4
	easy pedal	2	_____	

[a] Count the number of times you increase heart rate and decrease heart rate in a set period of time.

WORKOUT 43. WHO LET THE DOGS OUT?

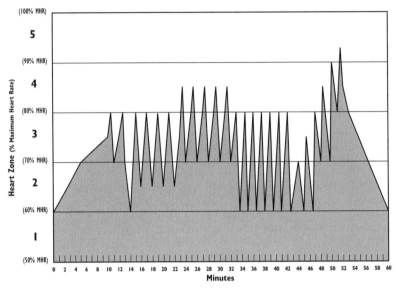

OVERVIEW

Poetry plays a part in our daily living and can extend into our cycling experience. David Whyte, in his poem "Working Together," wrote: "We shape our self / To fit this world / And by the world / Are shaped again" (from *The House of Belonging* [Many Rivers Press, 1998]). This is just what happens to our minds and our bodies as we get healthier and stronger. When we change, all things change.

As you quickly change focus when that unleashed dog is chasing you, mentally thank the pup for making you faster and fitter!

DESCRIPTION

The main emphasis of this workout is power and acceleration. On the 30-second sprints, use heavy resistance and a standing position as though you are being chased by dogs. One-minute recoveries between each interval provide for rest before the next dog chases you through another high-intensity interval. Accelerate as fast as you can until you reach the desired intensity, and then cling to it for the duration of the interval.

STATS AND TIPS FOR WORKOUT 43: WHO LET THE DOGS OUT?

Zone Number and Name	Minutes in Zone	Heart Zone Training Points	Estimated Calories
5. Red Line	2	10	30–40
4. Threshold	23	92	276–322
3. Aerobic	14	42	126–154
2. Temperate	21	42	126–168
1. Healthy Heart			
Totals	**60**	**186**	**558–684**

Tip: Efficient breathing makes for a better rider. Focus on your breathing, especially on forcing out expired air.

SEQUENCE FOR WORKOUT 43: WHO LET THE DOGS OUT?

Elapsed Time (min.)	Workout Plan	Heart Zone	Your Heart Rate (bpm)	Riding Time (min.)
0–10	Warm up to bottom of Z3, easy pedal	3	_____	10
10–14	[Increase HR to midpoint of Z3 (75%) in 30 sec., 90 rpm (9), (R) as needed. Increase HR to the bottom of Z4 (80%) in 30 sec., 90 rpm, add (R), followed by a 1 min. (rec) to bottom of Z3 (70%).] Repeat	3 4 3	_____ _____ _____	4
14–15	(Rec) to bottom of Z2 (60%)	2	_____	1
15–23	[Increase HR to bottom of Z4 (80%) in 1 min., 90 rpm (9), (R) as needed, followed by 1 min. (rec) to midpoint of Z2 (65%).] Repeat a total of 4 times	4 2	_____ _____	8
23–31	[From midpoint of Z2 increase HR to midpoint of Z3 in 30 sec., 90 rpm (9), (R) as needed. Increase HR to midpoint of Z4 (85%) in 30 sec., standing, 100 rpm (10), (R) as needed, followed by 1 min. (rec) to bottom of Z3 (70%).] Repeat a total of 4 times	3 4 3	_____ _____ _____	8
31–35	(Rec) to bottom of Z2 (60%). Stretch	2	_____	4
35–43	From bottom of Z2 (60%) sprint to bottom of Z4 (80%), then (rec) back down to the bottom of Z2 (60%). Count how many times you can do this work/recovery interval in 8 min.	2 4	_____ _____	8
43–44	1 min. (rec) bottom of Z2	2	_____	1
44–45.5	Increase HR to bottom of Z3 (70%) for 1 min. followed by 30 sec. (rec)	3	_____ _____	1.5
45.5–47	Increase HR to midpoint of Z3 (75%) for 1 min. followed by 30 sec. (rec)	3	_____	1.5
47–48.5	Increase HR to bottom of Z4 (80%) for 1 min. followed by 30 sec. (rec)	4	_____	1.5
48.5–50	Increase HR to midpoint of Z4 (85%) for 1 min. followed by 30 sec. (rec)	4	_____ _____	1.5
50–51.5	Increase HR to bottom of Z5 (90%) for 1 min. followed by 30 sec. (rec)	5	_____ _____	1.5
51.5–52.5	All-out effort to peak HR (90%+) for 1 min.	5	_____	1
52.5–54	Warm down to bottom of Z3, easy pedal	3	_____	1.5
54–60	Warm down to bottom of Z2, easy pedal	2	_____	6

WORKOUT 44. WINNER'S CIRCLE

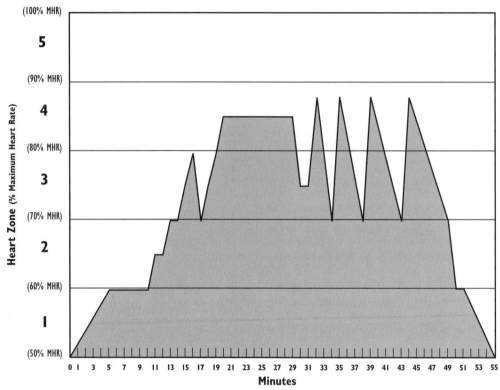

OVERVIEW

A winner uses an individualized training system to maximize her or his fitness in order to attain an "ideal performance state." To accomplish this, winning riders put all of the pieces of training together into a whole, a *winner's circle.* The winner's circle can be divided into different parts that include at least seven basic governing systems of training: specificity, overload, adaptation, balance, holism, psycho-emotionalism, and variability. Read about these seven parts to a training system in our companion book, *The Heart Rate Monitor Book for Outdoor and Indoor Cyclists* (VeloPress, 2000). Practice these different parts of training in the winner's circle by taking on the challenge to ride as many of these 50 workouts as you can.

DESCRIPTION

This is a great workout for building cycling-specific leg strength and muscular endurance for those long hill rides. Identify a specific heart rate number that you can sustain for an extended period of time. This number should be close to your anaerobic threshold heart rate. Select a heart rate high enough that you must reach to sustain it, but not so high that you can't sustain it for the duration of the work interval. Anaerobic threshold or lactic acid–threshold heart rate changes upward as you become more fit. Isolated-leg training teaches your legs to make smooth circles and also helps in the development of left- and right-leg power output at high cadences. Ultimately, though, getting yourself into your own Winner's Circle is the goal of training with the heart.

STATS AND TIPS FOR WORKOUT 44: WINNER'S CIRCLE

Zone Number and Name	Minutes in Zone	Heart Zone Training Points	Estimated Calories
5. Red Line			
4. Threshold	26	104	312–364
3. Aerobic	11	33	99–121
2. Temperate	10	20	60–80
1. Healthy Heart	8	8	24–40
Totals	**55**	**165**	**495–605**

Tip: Keep a training log or diary of your workouts. It's one of your most important training tools because it's your book, a report of your rides. Refer to the companion log book to this book series titled *The Heart Rate Monitor Log Book for Outdoor and Indoor Cyclists* (VeloPress, 2000).

SEQUENCE FOR WORKOUT 44: WINNER'S CIRCLE

Elapsed Time (min.)	Workout Plan	Heart Zone	Your Heart Rate (bpm)	Riding Time (min.)
0–5	Warm up to bottom of Z2, easy pedal	2	_____	5
5–10	[Isolated-leg training[a] (ILT): Right leg for 1 min., then left leg for 1 min.] Repeat a total of 2 times. Finish with both legs for 1 min.	3	_____	5
10–17	60 rpm (6) for 1 min., working on pedal stroke, then 70 rpm (7), for 1 min. and 80 rpm (8) for 1 min., increasing 10 rpm each min. up to 120 rpm (12) for a total of 7 min.	2 3 4	_____ _____ _____	7
17–18	(Rec) to bottom of Z3, easy pedal	3	_____	1
18–30	[(R), hard effort, 60 rpm (6) for 45 sec., last 15 sec. increase to 80 rpm (8).] Repeat a total of 12 times	4 4	_____ _____	12
30–32	(Rec) to bottom of Z3, easy pedal	3	_____	2
32–34	Increase HR to just below AT with (R), 80 rpm (8), seated	4	_____	2
34–35	(Rec) to midpoint of Z3 (75%), easy pedal	3	_____	1
35–38	Increase HR to just below AT with (R), 80 rpm (8), seated	4	_____	3
38–39	(Rec) to midpoint of Z3 (75%), easy pedal	3	_____	1
39–43	Increase HR to just below AT with (R), 80 rpm (8), seated	4	_____	4
43–44	(Rec) to midpoint of Z3 (75%), easy pedal	3	_____	1
44–49	Increase HR to just below AT with (R), 80 rpm (8), seated or standing	4	_____	5
49–50	(Rec) to midpoint of Z3 (75%), easy pedal	3	_____	1
50–52	Warm down to bottom of Z2, easy pedal	2	_____	2
52–55	Warm down to bottom of Z1, easy pedal	1	_____	3

[a] Pedaling with one leg at a time, resting the other on a box or stool. You may also choose to keep both feet in the pedals and allow one leg to relax while the other leg does the work.

WORKOUT 45. YOUR NUMBER'S UP

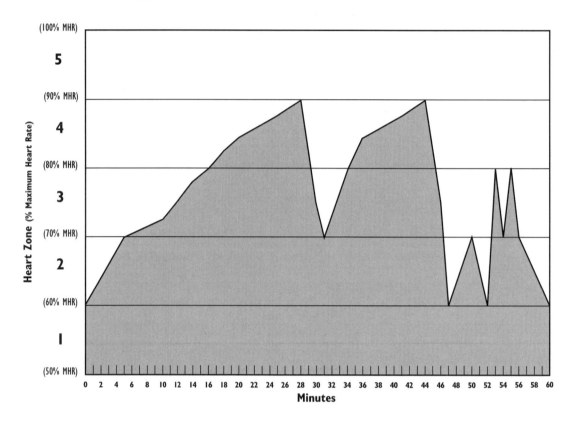

OVERVIEW

When your number is up, your number is up. That is what the cowboy gunslingers of the wild, wild West experienced as they rode their horses into the sunset. You are spared seeing that final finish line because when your number is up, you get a reprieve, and may you rest in peace.

DESCRIPTION

When you ride this workout, keep a lookout for your number to come up. That number is your anaerobic threshold heart rate number. If you are fit, this number is near the middle of Zone 4, the Threshold Zone. For many, it's 85% or more of your maximum heart rate. In this workout, when you see that number, stay within 5 bpm above or below it. The closer you can race at or above your anaerobic threshold—that is, the heart rate at which your body crosses over from fat burning to glycogen—the faster your speed. And, when your number is at your anaerobic threshold heart rate number, you are burning the maximum number of fat calories. Every additional calorie burned above this point comes from high-octane fuel, pure glycogen.

STATS AND TIPS FOR WORKOUT 45: YOUR NUMBER'S UP

Zone Number and Name	Minutes in Zone	Heart Zone Training Points	Estimated Calories
5. Red Line	4	20	60–80
4. Threshold	24	96	288–336
3. Aerobic	16	48	144–176
2. Temperate	16	32	96–128
1. Healthy Heart			
Totals	**60**	**196**	**588–720**

Tip: In order to estimate your anaerobic threshold heart rate, see Rule 15 in chapter 6.

SEQUENCE FOR WORKOUT 45: YOUR NUMBER'S UP

Elapsed Time (min.)	Workout Plan	Heart Zone	Your Heart Rate (bpm)	Riding Time (min.)
0–5	Warm up to bottom of Z2, easy pedal	2	_____	5
5–10	Increase HR to bottom of Z3	3	_____	5
10–12	From bottom of Z3 increase HR 5 bpm, choice	3	_____	2
12–14	Increase HR 5 bpm, choice	3	_____	2
14–16	Increase HR 5 bpm, choice	3	_____	2
16–18	Increase HR to bottom of Z4, choice	4	_____	2
18–20	From bottom of Z4 increase HR 5 bpm, choice	4	_____	2
20–25	Increase HR to 5 bpm below AT HR and sustain	4	_____	5
25–28	Increase HR to AT HR and sustain	4	_____	3
28–30	Increase HR 5 bpm above AT HR and sustain	4/5	_____	2
30–31	1 min. (rec) to bottom of Z3. Count the number of recovery beats	3	_____	1
31–34	3 min. (rec) to bottom of Z2, easy pedal	2	_____	3
34–36	Increase HR to bottom of Z4, choice	4	_____	2
36–52	Repeat min. 18–34	–	_____	16
52–55	Isolated-leg traning[a] (ILT): Right leg, 100 rpm (10) for 1 min., no (R), then left leg, 100 rpm (10) for 1 min., no (R). Then (rec) with both legs for 1 min.	3 2	_____ _____	3
55–57	Spin ups[b] at 60 rpm (6) to 120 rpm (12) for 1 min., (rec) for 1 min.	4 2	_____ _____	2
57–60	Warm down to bottom of Z2, easy pedal	2	_____	3

[a] Pedaling with one leg at a time, resting the other on a box or stool. You may also choose to keep both feet in the pedals and allow one leg to relax while the other leg does the work.
[b] Increasing cadence 5 to 10 rpm at regular intervals, keeping the pedal stroke smooth and efficient.

WORKOUT 46. THE SPINSTER

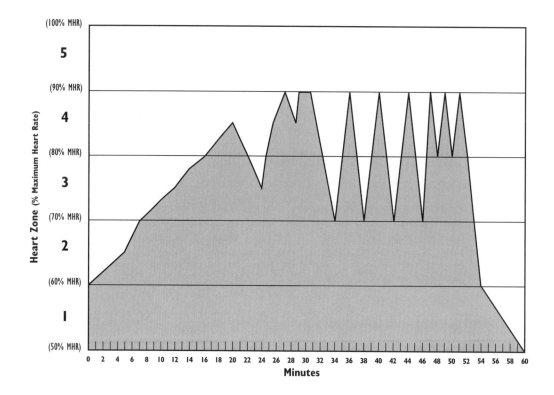

OVERVIEW

If you have the moxie not to settle on one target zone in your training, one workout in your repertoire, and one pedaling speed, then you qualify as a spinster. But as with any spinster, if you spend too much energy spinning, you too will get spent. That's what this workout is all about.

DESCRIPTION

This is a gradual warm up and spin up in which you can work on a smooth pedaling cadence and an efficient pedal stroke. Concentrate on pedaling with both legs equally, relaxing your upper body. Grip the handlebars lightly, keep your elbows slightly bent, knees directly over the pedal, and upper body quiet. Change

Empower your emotional heart by riding in the "flow" zone.

body positions at least every 5 minutes. Moving more forward on the saddle will work your quadriceps, and sliding toward the back of the saddle will work your hamstrings and glutes. During the sprint intervals, spin fast and smooth. Completely relax your legs on the recoveries. Spinster provides you with riding time in each of the five heart zones, so don't spend it all in just one.

STATS AND TIPS FOR WORKOUT 46: THE SPINSTER

Zone Number and Name	Minutes in Zone	Heart Zone Training Points	Estimated Calories
5. Red Line	14	70	210–280
4. Threshold	13	52	156–182
3. Aerobic	22	66	198–242
2. Temperate	9	18	54–72
1. Healthy Heart	2	2	6–10
Totals	**60**	**208**	**624–786**

Tip: Pedal in circles to create an even distribution of force through the stroke.

SEQUENCE FOR WORKOUT 46: THE SPINSTER

Elapsed Time (min.)	Workout Plan	Heart Zone	Your Heart Rate (bpm)	Riding Time (min.)
0–5	Warm up to bottom of Z2, easy pedal	2	_____	5
5–7	Increase HR to midpoint of Z2, 70 rpm (7)	2	_____	2
7–10	Increase HR to bottom of Z3, 80 rpm (8)	3	_____	3
10–12	Increase HR 5 bpm, 90 rpm (9)	3	_____	2
12–14	Increase HR 5 bpm, 100 rpm (10)	3	_____	2
14–16	Increase HR 5 bpm, 110 rpm (11)	3	_____	2
16–18	Increase HR 5 bpm, 120 rpm (12), add (R) as needed	4	_____	2
18–20	Increase HR 5 bpm, 130 rpm (13), add (R) as needed	4	_____	2
20–22	Increase HR 5 bpm, 140 rpm (14), add (R) as needed	4	_____	2
22–24	(Rec) to bottom of Z3, easy pedal	3	_____	2
24–34	[15 sec. sprint, 15 sec. (rec) 30 sec. sprint, 30 sec. (rec) 45 sec. sprint, 45 sec. (rec) 60 sec. sprint, 60 sec. (rec)] Repeat a total of 2 times	3 4 5	_____ _____ _____	10
34–36	(Rec) to bottom of Z3	3	_____	2
36–48	Ups and downs[a] from bottom of Z3 to bottom of Z5, choice. Count the number of times in 12 min.	3 5	_____	12
48–49	Sustain bottom of Z4	4	_____	1
49–54	Ups and downs from bottom of Z4 to bottom of Z5, choice	4 5	_____	5
54–60	Warm down to bottom of Z1, easy pedal	1	_____	6

[a] Count the number of times you increase heart rate and decrease heart rate in a set period of time.

Workout 47. Surge

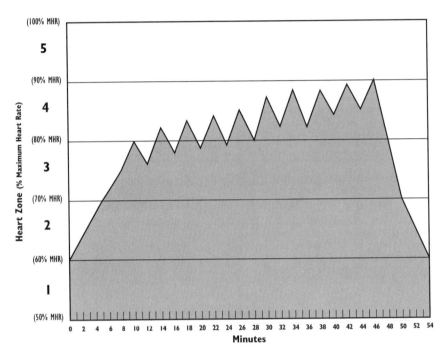

Overview

The best athletic club or training gym in the world is life itself. Every moment that we breathe gives us a chance to practice getting better at breathing. Likewise, every moment that we ride gives us a chance to practice getting fitter and healthier and to perform better on the bike. Basically, life is a terrific gym because it gives us the present moment to practice living by riding our bike. If you want to get better on the bike, then use every opportunity you have to practice and ride the bike. Riding the workout Surge is just that opportunity. Practice Surge and watch your cycling get better.

Description

The goal of this workout is to reach the finish line (Zone 5) with surges of effort followed by short intervals of rest. The surges of power will recruit your fast-twitch muscles and develop strength. Much of the time your heart rate is above 75% of your maximum heart rate, so you are training both your

Stats and Tips for Workout 47: Surge

Zone Number and Name	Minutes in Zone	Heart Zone Training Points	Estimated Calories
5. Red Line	2	10	30–40
4. Threshold	30	120	360–420
3. Aerobic	15	45	135–165
2. Temperate	7	14	42–56
1. Healthy Heart			
Totals	54	189	567–681

Tip: Place the heart rate monitor on the handlebars and focus on your heart rate.

aerobic and anaerobic systems. Use resistance or big gears to surge ahead and in front of the pack. A fundamental rule for living life in the best gym in the world is "Don't cause pain" (Sylvia Boorstein, *It's Easier Than You Think: The Buddhist Way to Happiness* [Harper, San Francisco, 1995, p. 41]). The workout Surge violates that fundamental rule. Life is painful, yet suffering is optional. Just don't suffer too much during this 60-minute ride on the best athletic workout—your life and your bike.

SEQUENCE FOR WORKOUT 47: SURGE

Elapsed Time (min.)	Workout Plan	Heart Zone	Your Heart Rate (bpm)	Riding Time (min.)
0–5	Warm up to bottom of Z2, easy pedal	2	_____	5
5–8	Increase HR to bottom of Z3, choice	3	_____	3
8–10	Increase HR to midpoint of Z3 (75%), (R)	3	_____	2
10–12	Increase HR to bottom of Z4, cadence **Note: Min. 12–48 include a series of (8) 2 min. recoveries along with (8) 2 min. surges of energy and increased HR**	4	_____	2
12–14	From bottom of Z4 decrease HR 8 bpm and sustain	3	_____	2
14–16	Surge ahead in intensity by increasing HR 10 bpm, (R)	4	_____	2
16–18	Decrease HR 8 bpm and sustain	3	_____	2
18–20	Surge ahead by increasing HR 10 bpm, (R)	4	_____	2
20–22	Decrease HR 8 bpm and sustain	3	_____	2
22–24	Surge ahead by increasing HR 10 bpm, (R)	4	_____	2
24–26	Decrease HR 8 bpm and sustain	3/4	_____	2
26–28	Surge ahead by increasing HR 10 bpm, (R)	4	_____	2
28–30	Decrease HR to bottom of Z4 and sustain	4	_____	2
30–32	Surge ahead by increasing HR 10 bpm, (R)	4	_____	2
32–34	Decrease HR by 8 bpm and sustain	4	_____	2
34–36	Surge ahead by increasing HR 10 bpm, (R)	4	_____	2
36–38	Decrease HR by 8 bpm and sustain	4	_____	2
38–40	Surge ahead by increasing HR 10 bpm, (R)	4	_____	2
40–42	Decrease HR by 8 bpm and sustain	4	_____	2
42–44	Surge ahead by increasing HR 10 bpm, (R)	4	_____	2
44–46	Decrease HR by 8 bpm and sustain	4	_____	2
46–48	Surge ahead by increasing HR 10 bpm, (R)	4/5	_____	2
48–50	Decrease HR to bottom of Z4	4	_____	2
50–54	Decrease HR and warm down to Z3 then to bottom of Z2	3 2	_____	4

WORKOUT 48. HANG ON! HELP IS ON THE WAY!

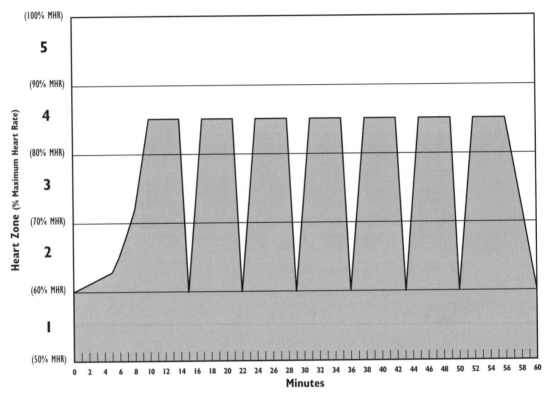

OVERVIEW

Clinging to your old habits on the bike can be dangerous, but now is the time. If you hang on to the intervals, your relief is moments away. Relief to a heart zone trainer is recovery. There are different ways of recovering that lower heart rate. By now, you should be able to name them but here are a few: decreasing resistance, slowing cadence, changing body position, changing environmental conditions (temperature, humidity, wind factors, etc.), and changing emotional and mental focus. Hang on any way you can and use all of the tricks that you have to recover as quickly as you possibly can.

DESCRIPTION

The goal of some types of endurance riding and racing is to stay just under your anaerobic threshold heart rate. By training at a heart rate number that's below your anaerobic threshold heart rate, you can usually avoid falling into a deep and dark hole. Known in the famed Hawaiian Ironman triathlon as "the pit," this is a place in your physiology where there is insufficient oxygen to sustain the intensity. When you are in the pit, your training or racing intensity results in the production of more lactic acid than your metabolic pathway's ability to remove it, as exercise physiologists explain. Repeatedly completing the workout Hang On! improves your lactic acid–clearance systems, develops your cardiovascular system to utilize oxygen more efficiently, and gives you the satisfaction that you can hang on even when the riding gets tougher.

STATS AND TIPS FOR WORKOUT 48: HANG ON! HELP IS ON THE WAY!

Zone Number and Name	Minutes in Zone	Heart Zone Training Points	Estimated Calories
5. Red Line			
4. Threshold	35	140	420–490
3. Aerobic	2	6	18–22
2. Temperate	23	46	138–184
1. Healthy Heart			
Totals	**60**	**192**	**576–696**

Tip: Enter your anaerobic threshold heart rate number into your log book and in a month try this workout again. Has your anaerobic threshold gone up or down? If you are getting fitter, what direction should your anaerobic threshold heart rate move?

SEQUENCE FOR WORKOUT 48: HANG ON! HELP IS ON THE WAY!

Elapsed Time (min.)	Workout Plan	Heart Zone	Your Heart Rate (bpm)	Riding Time (min.)
0–5	Increase HR to bottom of Z2, easy pedal	2	_____	5
5–10	Increase HR 5 bpm every min. with cadence (rpm)	2	_____	5
		2	_____	
		2	_____	
		3	_____	
		3	_____	
10–15	Increase HR to just *below* AT[a] and sustain	4	_____	5
15–17	(Rec) to bottom of Z2	2	_____	2
17–22	Increase HR to just *below* AT and sustain	4	_____	5
22–24	(Rec) to bottom of Z2	2	_____	2
24–29	Increase HR to just *below* AT and sustain	4	_____	5
29–31	(Rec) to bottom of Z2	2	_____	2
31–36	Increase HR to just *below* AT and sustain	4	_____	5
36–38	(Rec) to bottom of Z2	2	_____	2
38–43	Increase HR to just *below* AT and sustain	4	_____	5
43–45	(Rec) to bottom of Z2	2	_____	2
45–50	Increase HR to just *below* AT and sustain	4	_____	5
50–52	(Rec) to bottom of Z2	2	_____	2
52–57	Increase HR to just *below* AT and sustain	4	_____	5
57–60	Warm down to bottom of Z2	2	_____	3

[a] A heart rate goal that is just under your estimated anaerobic threshold or the heart rate at which you crossover from aerobic to anaerobic metabolism. Note the anaerobic threshold test in Rule 15 in chapter 6.

WORKOUT 49. ESCAPE FROM THE ROCK

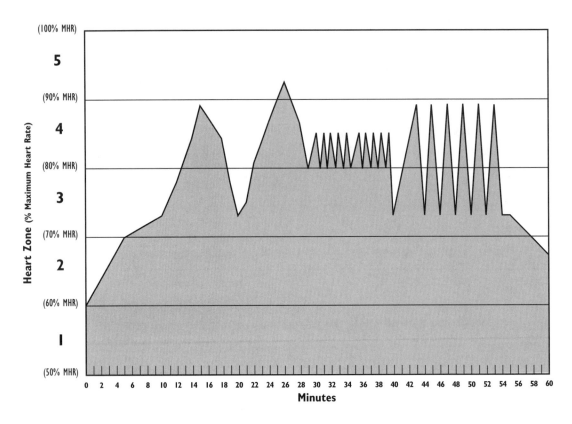

OVERVIEW

Escape from the Rock is a television-premiered triathlon race in the city where you can leave your heart, as Tony Bennett would sing—San Francisco. The race attracts some of the best triathletes in the world. The racers achieve high heart rates as they fight to swim through the frigid currents of San Francisco Bay. Then, after a brief run to warm their core temperature, they bike up the steep hills of Marin County. The winning female and the winning male are individuals who can endure and conquer the challenges the course has to offer. Jean-Jacques Rousseau once said, "To endure is the first thing that a child ought to learn, and that which they will have the most need to know." You will find this 60-minute blast of intervals with fast changes of 10 and 30 bpm your escape from your rock.

DESCRIPTION

The first half of this workout is a variation on a 10-bpm interval. You have 30 to 60 seconds to accomplish the intensity changes; thus you drive your heart muscle to quickly respond to the changing workload and recovery phases. Like being a prisoner on Alcatraz Island, "The Rock," you begin to fatigue as the workload gets harder. There is nothing like a tough set of intervals to get you fit enough to break out, or as we say in cycling, "break away." Always, by digging deep to keep up the pace, you can survive your internment, this workout.

STATS AND TIPS FOR WORKOUT 49: ESCAPE FROM THE ROCK

Zone Number and Name	Minutes in Zone	Heart Zone Training Points	Estimated Calories
5. Red Line	2	10	30–40
4. Threshold	27	108	324–378
3. Aerobic	22	66	198–242
2. Temperate	9	18	54–72
1. Healthy Heart			
Totals	60	202	606–732

Tip: Planning your workouts is important. Plan your work and work your plan.

SEQUENCE FOR WORKOUT 49: ESCAPE FROM THE ROCK

Elapsed Time (min.)	Workout Plan	Heart Zone	Your Heart Rate (bpm)	Riding Time (min.)
0–5	Warm up to bottom of Z2 (60%), easy pedal	2	_____	5
5–10	Increase HR minus bottom of Z3, with cadence/rpm	3	_____	5
10–12	Increase HR to max. HR minus 50 bpm	3	_____	2
12–18	From max. HR of 50 bpm, increase HR 10 bpm every 2 min. (3 times), choice	3 4 4	_____ _____ _____	6
18–21	Decrease HR 10 bpm every min. for 3 min.	4 3 3	_____ _____ _____	3
21–22	Increase HR 5 bpm, choice	3	_____	1
22–28	Increase HR 10 bpm every 2 min. (3 times), choice	3/4 4 5	_____ _____ _____	6
28–29	Decrease HR to midpoint of Z4	4	_____	1
29–30	Decrease HR to bottom of Z4	4	_____	1
30–40	[Increase HR to midpoint of Z4 in 30 sec., then decrease HR to bottom of Z4 in 30 sec.] Repeat a total of 10 times	4 4	_____ _____	10
40–43	(Rec) to max. HR minus 50 bpm, sustain	3	_____	3
43–55	[From max. HR minus 50 bpm, increase HR 30 bpm for 1 min., choice, then decrease HR 30 bpm for 1 min.] Repeat a total of 6 times	4 3	_____ _____	12
55–60	Warm down to bottom of Z2, easy pedal	2	_____	5

WORKOUT 50. THE FINAL ANSWER

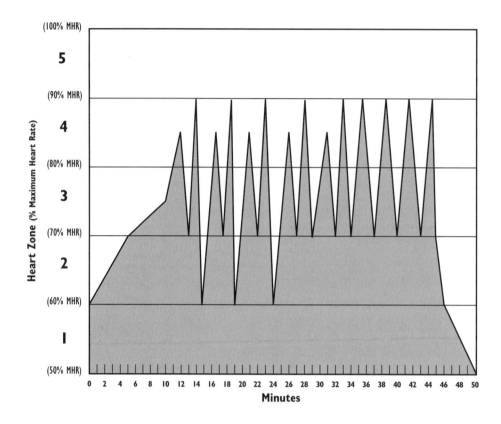

OVERVIEW

There are some people who, as we say in Heart Zones Cycling, "get it." That means they understand the training principles, and most importantly, they apply the information. Nancy Weninger is one of those people who believed in Heart Zones Cycling, used her heart rate monitor as a testing and biofeedback tool, and systematically set out to prove over one year's time that she was getting fitter. As you can see from her training chart, in January 2000, Nancy was riding indoors on her trainer at 19 miles per hour and with a heart rate of 170 bpm. In February her heart rate had dropped to 160 bpm while she was riding at 19 miles per hour and doing exactly the same indoor protocol. As you can see, her heart rate continued to drop through the year, and in November she was riding at 19 miles an hour at a heart rate of 140 bpm. In less than one year's time, that is a 30-bpm drop. The proof is in the numbers! Nancy can now ride at 24 miles an hour at 170 bpm compared to a year ago when she could only ride that heart rate at 19 miles an hour. She is getting fitter and faster and having more fun!

If Nancy were asked, "What's your final answer regarding training?" she would say, "Training by heart rate works!"

The Final Answer workout is dedicated to athletes like Nancy who are motivated to apply what they know.

Nancy Weninger's Bike Time Trial Chart

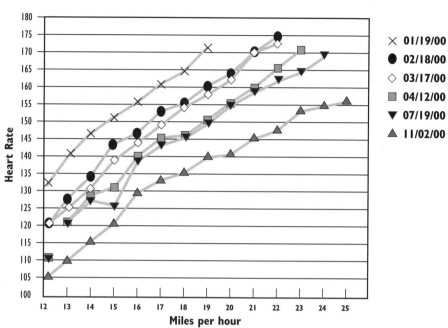

×	01/19/00
●	02/18/00
◇	03/17/00
▣	04/12/00
▼	07/19/00
▲	11/02/00

Description

This workout is a series of hills to make you stronger, sprints to make you faster, and recoveries to prepare you for more to come. The 30-second and 60-second sprints will give you a chance to put the pedal to the metal and go for your peak heart rate. That is the highest heart rate number on your monitor for the workout. Go for the gusto and don't be surprised if your heart rate continues to increase for a few seconds after you finish the sprint. There is a lag time or update time of 3 to 5 seconds on most monitors. The final answer will be 12 minutes of intervals with 40-bpm changes when you legs are fatigued and your motivation is dwindling. Hang in there and make your final answer finishing the workout.

Stats and Tips for Workout 50: The Final Answer

Zone Number and Name	Minutes in Zone	Heart Zone Training Points	Estimated Calories
5. Red Line	10	50	150–200
4. Threshold	5	20	60–70
3. Aerobic	21	63	189–231
2. Temperate	12	24	72–96
1. Healthy Heart	2	2	6–10
Totals	**50**	**159**	**477–607**

Tip: Lead your heart rate by 3–5 bpm so that you don't shoot over the heart rate goal.

SEQUENCE FOR WORKOUT 50: THE FINAL ANSWER

Elapsed Time (min.)	Workout Plan	Heart Zone	Your Heart Rate (bpm)	Riding Time (min.)
0–5	Warm up to bottom of Z2, easy pedal	2	_____	5
5–10	Increase HR to bottom of Z3, cadence/rpm	3	_____	5
10–12	Increase HR to midpoint of Z3, choice	3	_____	2
	Note: Min. 12–46 include a series of hills, sprints, and recoveries			
12–26	[Increase HR to midpoint of Z4 using heavy (R) or hard gearing and 70 rpm (7) for 1 min., then (rec) to bottom of Z3 with easy pedal for 1 min. After (rec) increase HR to bottom of Z5 or peak HR, with all-out 30 sec. sprint, then (rec) to bottom of Z2 for 2 min., easy pedal.] Repeat a total of 3 times	4 3 5 2	_____ _____ _____ _____	14
26–34	[Increase HR to midpoint of Z4 using moderate (R) or medium gearing and 90 rpm (9) for 1 min., then (rec) to bottom of Z3 with easy pedal for 1 min. After (rec) increase HR to bottom of Z5 or peak HR with all-out 1 min. sprint, then (rec) to bottom of Z3 for 1 min, easy pedal.] Repeat	4 3 5 5	_____ _____ _____ _____	8
34–46	Ups and downs:[a] Increase HR from bottom of Z3 to bottom of Z5 followed by a (rec) to bottom of Z3, choice. Count the number of times you can do this up and down interval in 12 min., choice. This will be your "final answer."	3 5 3	_____ _____ _____	12
46–50	Warm down to bottom of Z2, easy pedal 2	2	_____	4

[a] Typically 30- or 40-bpm increases in intensity with a recovery back to the starting point. Count the number of times you increase your heart rate and recover in a set period of time. Usually your choice on how you want to raise intensity. Recoveries should be active; keep pedaling easily.

Be sure to rest between workouts.

Chapter 7
Going Beyond: Growing Your Fitness, Growing Your Life

As we conclude these fifty Heart Zones Cycling workouts, we have one last tip or you—it's about finding the fountain of youth. When explorers went looking for the fountain of youth in centuries past, usually they simply found abundant amounts of bloodthirsty mosquitoes, as well as untimely ends. Today there are many who are still searching for fountains of youth and still coming to untimely ends, but currently the vast number of untimely deaths are from the effects of inactivity—too much stress, obesity, and degenerative diseases—rather than from a perilous journey.

One of the best ways we know to avoid an untimely end is to be active, and the secret to staying active is to continue learning and setting goals for yourself *and* to use your heart as the center of your training program. Heart Zone Training is a member of your support team for a lifetime of health and happiness.

Learning can happen in many ways, and we encourage you to continue on your exploration of fitness and challenge you to try new workouts. "When was the last time you did something for the first time?" is one of the questions we constantly ask ourselves and hope that you ask yourself as well. Doing anything for the first time means you will need to invest in taking the time to learn what to do. As you learn something new, you become empowered by conviction and determination, which enables you to reach fruition through action and effort. Keep growing your riding and training experiences for life.

Remember the four parts to training success from the first chapter? They are: (1) an effective training program and training *plan,* (2) the *inspiration* and motivation to train, whether from well-defined personal goals or the sheer pleasure of training, (3) *support* for learning about training, and (4) feedback on your *results* throughout the training process. With a plan, inspiration, and support, you should be able to see the results of your efforts.

We hope we have achieved our goal of giving you a big dose of learning support in this book and maybe even some inspiration! For complete details on planning workouts and training with a heart rate monitor—and for further inspiration!—read our other books in the Heart Zone Training Series. The first book, *The Heart Rate Monitor Book for Outdoor and Indoor Cyclists*, gives you more information on all aspects of getting where you want to go with Heart Zones Cycling.

Our second book, *The Heart Rate Monitor Log Book*, gives you a place to record your journey. Writing down your goals and progress in your training program is one of the easiest ways to stay motivated, focused, and inspired, and it is something most athletes rely on. Professional athletes would not waste a minute of their time if keeping a log book didn't make a huge difference to their success.

Stay motivated by learning, growing, and taking on new challenges. A large dose of inspiration helps keep you motivated and the best inspiration we know of is the most purely internal—set a goal and accomplish it. Get support. Your friends, family, training partners, workmates, and clubs are all excellent support groups. Finally, when we receive positive feedback, we stay motivated. Use that heart rate monitor, with all of its power, as a feedback tool.

When was the last time you did something for the first time? Ride all fifty workouts in this book, and you will have answered that question.

Afterword
A Change of Heart

Todd was raised on a potato farm in Idaho. When he left the farm to pursue a profession in music and real estate sales, he became totally inactive, sedentary. The wake-up call arrived when he found he was short of breath from climbing a few stairs. In addition, his clothes just didn't fit. Twenty pounds heavier than his healthy weight, with about 28% body fat, Todd knew it was time to change his lifestyle. He joined a club and started something new—an indoor cycling class.

At first it was hard to stay on the program of riding three times a week. To keep motivated, Todd decided to set a training goal. His new friends from the Heart Zones Cycling class he was taking were doing a 100-mile bike tour, and he thought that sounded both fun and challenging. Todd knew that if he didn't fill out the entry blank and send in his registration fee he wouldn't be committed. It set him back financially $30. It set him forward emotionally thousands of dollars. There was a date on a calendar for him to train towards. Commitment. There was a goal. Determination. Because he lived in the high, cold country, snow kept him from riding outdoors, so he did most of his riding indoors. During the training time he also fell in love with his studio bike, his heart rate monitor, and even more in love with his wife and family and, ultimately, with himself.

As is the case with many people, he returned to his sedentary ways after the 100-mile ride, starting and quitting several exercise programs, yo-yo dieting, and gaining more weight. He finally came to the conclusion at the age of forty-eight that it was worth another try. What helped him make the decision was something called "hitting the convergence threshold." The convergence threshold is an intersection in your life's roadway. It is a place and time when negative events and emotions accumulate and converge, resulting in a need for a dramatic change.

For Todd, it was a convergence of physical problems. He had his appendix removed. He was popping pills—high blood pressure pills and beta blockers for his irregular heart beat. He was diagnosed with sleep apnea. Todd bottomed out. With six grandchildren, a wonderful marriage, and memories of how great he used to feel and how much energy he used to have, the energy of change intersected. Other events transpired at the same time, which helped to put him over the threshold and motivate him to change. Todd hit an all-time-high weight—220 pounds resting dormant on a frame built to carry 170.

It's been two months since Todd started his heart zone training program, Heart Zones Cycling. He's dropped 10 pounds, written a three-year goal plan, read several books on heart zone training, uses his heart rate monitor for every workout, and taken up cross-country skiing for cross-training. Last year, his wife bought him a trainer to ride indoors at home, and he's fallen in love with it. Finally, he broke down and bought a new heart rate monitor that downloads into his personal computer.

Todd, who goes by the self-selected nickname "Spud," may have grown up on a potato farm, but he sure isn't a couch potato any longer. He's getting fitter and fitter every day. And you can, too.

One way is to stay in touch with us. If you have any problems getting started on this program just contact us at www.heartzones.com and we will answer your question, give you a dose of motivation, or like we did for Todd, help you get back on the bike, the road, and living the lifestyle of taking good care of your heart. After all, isn't that what you want?

About the Authors

Sally Edwards is a member of the Triathlon Hall of Fame, an author of fifteen sports training books, a sixteen-time Ironman finisher, and a former master's world record holder. She also serves as national spokeswoman for the Danskin Women's Triathlon Series, and since 1990, she has finished every one, mostly in last place, staying back to encourage the slowest across the finish line.

Sally is also one of the world's leading advocates of using heart rate monitors in training. In addition to co-authoring with Sally Reed the other titles in this series—*The Heart Rate Monitor Book* and *The Heart Rate Monitor Log Book*—she has written several other books on the subject, including: *Heart Zones Cycling Master Trainer Manual for Indoor Cycle Instructors; Heart Zone Training; The Heart Rate Monitor Guidebook to Heart Zone Training; Heart Rate Monitor Book for Physical Education: Middle Schools;* and *Heart Rate Monitor Book for Physical Education: High Schools.*

Sally Edwards heads up Heart Zones, a company focused on heart rate training and heart rate monitors, and also coaches elite athletes, runs her own consulting business, and is a frequent keynote speaker at conventions and meetings.

Her athletic resume includes college intercollegiate athletics and an appearance in the 1984 U.S. Olympic Trials marathon. Her career as a businesswoman began when she founded the Fleet Feet chain of retail sports stores in 1976.

Sally's real passions are to get more women involved in sports and fitness activities and to help first-timers cross the finish line. She believes that anyone and everyone can get fit and experience the boost in self-esteem that accompanies the effort.

Most of all, she cares that no matter which race you run, you show up at the starting line with a smile on your face and cross the finish line with a bigger one. Sally lives in Sacramento, California, with her Australian cattle dog, Allez Allez.

Sally Reed, M.A., is the athletic director of the prestigious Bellevue Club in Bellevue, Washington. More importantly, in 1997, she single-handedly created the Heart Zones Cycling training system. After attending one Heart Zones Training seminar, she designed, wrote, and started teaching the first Heart Zones Cycling programs that are the basis of this book.

For the past three years, she has traveled around the country writing, speaking, certifying, and teaching seminars, workshops, camps, and programs on Heart Zones Cycling. She has written over a hundred workouts using a heart rate monitor on a bike as well as a manual for cycling coaches and instructors to become certified, titled *The Blue Jersey Master Trainers Manual for Heart Zones Cycling.*

She is a former world-class skier, a competitive triathlete, and an endurance cyclist. But more importantly, at fifty-three years old, she has four grandchildren and lives with her husband, Scott, in Issaquah, Washington.

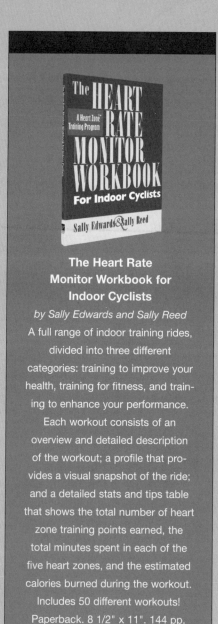
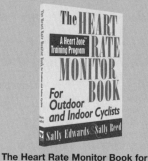

138